M000286406

THROUGH

Fire AND *Rain*

Surviving the Impossible with Love, Music, and Precision Medicine

MaryAnn *and* Joseph Anselmo

WITH Lisa Cerasoli

STORY MERCHANT BOOKS

STORY MERCHANT BOOKS · LOS ANGELES · 2016

Through Fire and Rain

Copyright © 2016 by MaryAnn and Joseph Anselmo. All rights reserved.

No part of this book may be reproduced or transmitted in any form or by any means, electronic or mechanical, including photocopying, recording, or by any information storage and retrieval system, without the express written permission of the author.

ISBN-13: 978-0-9981628-1-2

Story Merchant Books
400 S. Burnside Ave. #11B,
Los Angeles, CA 90036
http://www.storymerchant.com/books.html

Interior Design: Danielle Canfield
Cover: Dafeenah Jamal, www.IndieDesignz.com

THROUGH

Fire

AND Rain

MARYANN *and* JOSEPH ANSELMO

WITH LISA CERASOLI

The Bungalow Foundation

The Bungalow Foundation is a public charity that funds bio-medical Precision Medicine Initiatives by way of grants to post-doctoral and clinical research fellows working with academic, medical or research institutions.

Founded by Joseph and MaryAnn Anselmo in 2012

www.thebungalow.org

TIME

Both of these women have brain tumors.

One is beating the odds.

CLOSING THE **CANCER GAP**

BY ALICE PARK

MARCH 2015

"I've never thought of myself as a strong person.... After all, I'm just a jazz singer."

—MaryAnn "Mariel" Larsen Anselmo

THROUGH *Fire* AND *Rain*

PART I:

Fire

one

MaryAnn

IT WAS A SOLD-OUT SHOW at Chico's House of Jazz. I was minutes from going on. Everything was perfect. I was finally sure of myself. Thousands of hours of vocal coaching sessions, rehearsals, and studio sessions to make a good first release was all worth it. I was ready to unveil my hard work to the world. The arrangements were solid and the band was excellent. I was what they call prepared. I had been ready for this moment all my life.

When you're a kid and they say you have a special talent, you think: *when I grow up, that's what I'll do—get paid to sing, dance, juggle.* Whatever your talent was, that's what you were going to do.

"I wanna be a vet, or a fireman, or a school teacher." When I was swinging from the monkey bars at St. Patrick's Elementary, that's what all the kids talked about. Then they grew up, and after a

few years of school, they became those things—doctors, fire-fighters, teachers. But I had a special "tal-ent." I sang. I wanted to be a singer when I grew up. You don't major in that then fill out applications, interview for a permanent position, get hired, and start two weeks from Monday. Establishing a singing career is a little different.

But here I was, making it. The house was packed. Everyone was waiting for me.

⟋⟍

"Turn down that music, Artie!" Mom hollered. "The Spanish Flea Again? How do you even sing to that?"

Dad made a funny face.

Then Mom instructed, "Just put her on the chair, Artie!"

My mom had no idea that it was her little girl who was listening to Herb Alpert & the Tijuana Brass, one of the best trumpet players in the world. Dad was training my ears for rhythm! But he did as Mom had instructed, and put me on one of our new red vinyl chairs from A&S.

Then he handed me a soup ladle. "Why don't you start with 'Fools Rush In,' sweetheart. You know how your mother feels about that one," he whispered with a wink.

"Sing 'Fools Rush In' for me, darling!" Mom chimed in, snatching Dad's thoughts and making them her own.

It hardly mattered what I sang, whether it be an Al Martino number or a snappy tune like "Baby Face" by Whispering Jack Smith (that was Aunt Lil's song).

On Sundays, the family got together to play cards and sing. I wasn't the only one with a voice. My father, Artie (as most people knew him), had a voice that would melt butter straight from the icebox, like Vaughn Monroe's but better. And Grandma Agnes stopped the show—or the card game—whenever she'd belt out "Sunny Side of the Street" by Louis Armstrong. My voice was smooth like Peggy Lee's, or so they'd muse. In a time when the Beatles were coming fast and hard onto the music scene in the early sixties, Peggy Lee was my idol. We were all about the American Standards in our red brick townhouse on Prospect Street in Park Slope, Brooklyn. Someday I hoped to be compared to her, to hear my songs on the radio and the DJ announce, "UP next: the sultry, effort-free vocal stylings of MaryAnn. Stay tuned!"

———————— ✌ ————————

I wasn't twenty-one, or even thirty-one anymore. In my twenties I was singing on a stage all right, but it wasn't for a sold-out show at Chico's House of Jazz, the premiere New Jersey venue for emerging and national jazz artists. I was at the Playboy Resort & Country Club, serving guests and singing backup in the playmate lounge.

I took pride in being selected as a bunny. It was a job I found exciting and financially rewarding and it gave me an opportunity to meet other aspiring singers, as well as the headliner acts that performed live on Friday and Saturday nights in the Cabaret Room. Just the exposure to a live entertainment environment taught me so much about stagecraft and how to sing for live audiences. I'd clear at least $200 a night or more on the floor. This was in the late seventies and that kind of take-home was a big deal for a young woman without any formal education. If I sang instead of served, I'd take home considerably less money, but the sacrifice was well worth it.

Everything about the early days of my music career felt lucky. I had been picking up a few bucks in tips at the Jorgensens' Inn in Vernon, New Jersey before the Playboy Resort. That's when I waited on two women who read my nametag and said, "MaryAnn, sweetheart, you ought to be anywhere but here." And they recommended I apply to work at the Playboy Resort.

I met Ricky Nelson and Bobby Rydell there while posing as a bunny and doling out cocktails to packed audiences during their shows. This led to my first professional vocal coach in New York City: Carlo Menotti at Carnegie Hall Studios, and then the well-known pop/rock voice trainer Marty Lawrence. I was still doing

American Standards from my childhood and singing pop back then. *What did I know?* Marty was brilliant and so was his son, Don Lawrence, my new vocal coach who worked with me on song material. I have never been disillusioned about the hard work that goes into a singing or any successful career. I was excited to be just a back up vocalist in the lounge at the Playboy Club in Great Gorge, and to be working with an esteemed vocal coach. Stardom wasn't exactly hunting me down, but it was sniffling around. I was discovering my voice and myself.

I eventually left the club for a regular job in sales. I wanted to be taken seriously and I feared that the bunny suit would have hindered that. Getting my "voice in the door" locally in the clubs in NYC was my target goal. I hadn't settled on an image, though. By this point it was the early nineties. Time sure flies when you're pursuing your dream.

I remember being at a hair salon on 5th, getting ready for a gig, when a prominent music producer approached me like I was a long lost cousin. He knew about me through my voice trainer and mentor. Maybe he heard my demo recording of Patsy Cline's version of "Crazy." Anyway, he talked fast about "possibilities" and ended with, "I produced *Ingènue* with K.D. Lang. You ought to move to Nashville. That's what you need to do. And look me up when you get there. You're a Country Western singer. You just don't know it yet." Then he slipped me his card and vanished before I could soak it all in.

He must have heard me perform "Constant Craving." How I loved to cover that tune—the lyrics so sincere, the melody smoldering. The audience went nuts whenever I sang it. I knew that fusing country with blues and jazz was what I was trying to create for myself and my future, but my vision wasn't refined enough yet, for I hadn't broken free from the local pack of "singers for hire." I didn't believe that Nashville would be where my passion for music would flourish and my vision would merge, though. So I stayed in New York.

In 1996, Diana Krall was nominated for her first Grammy for *All for You: A Dedication to the Nat King Cole Trio, her third album*. It was nice to see a talent like her get that kind of recognition.

The hurdle I was continuously leaping over was my day job in sales. At that time, I was earning a living as an advertising consultant for Verizon Yellow Pages. It wasn't exactly my lifelong dream of performing to a sold-out audience at Carnegie Hall, but it paid the bills, as well as vocal lessons, studio time, and musicians. The people at my day job didn't support my career. I told white lies about what I was doing with my free time. I have no idea what my longtime associates did when they were off the clock and fortunately it was far away from the local music scene. I rarely saw any of them out. That helped keep me stay undercover.

Even though my career had been moseying along laterally, my love life had skyrocketed into the dazzling stars when I married Joe Anselmo on May 7th *and* June 8th of 1994. (More on that later!)

Love, as love does, brought new energy to everything. Joe's businesses were booming with the economy. I was discovering my genre was classified as jazz. It was where I belonged, especially with Diana Krall so hot on the scene. I felt connected to that kind of music. And I had started writing, too.

"Through Fire and Rain" was one of my first collaborative efforts. I've heard writers say they've channeled stories and song lyrics. I experienced that sensation with "Through Fire and Rain." I didn't realize then that the song would foreshadow my future.

At one point, my father gave me a substantial loan to hire a marketing team, who mapped out my future. I still have it all in a PowerPoint. It's gorgeous. Then the company vanished into thin air. It was a pretty decent pathway to success in theory, I've been told. I don't know if it was worth ten grand, though. I'm not kidding even a little bit when I say that love made everything okay at the end of the day. I had Joe. I had a wonderful father. I had a beautiful son, Dustin, who was the light of my life. He was an up-and-coming filmmaker and photographer, making his stamp as an artist, just like me. We were soaring to the top together. I wasn't a girl anymore and my career hadn't gone "as planned" but who has time for self-pity? Not me. I adored the parallels between my career and Dustin's; I thought it was cool that our careers were galloping toward the sunrise of success in sync. Leaving music behind has never crossed my mind, so this was me looking on the bright side, I guess. Over the years I've learned to trust the human desire to experience greatness in others, even more than I trust my own intuition. The world was rooting for my success as strongly as Joe and I were rooting for Dustin's. I incorporated that notion into my pre-show mantra, which has been a real nerve-calmer for me. Plus, my debut album was receiving accolades and stirring confidence anew.

"...This intimate portrait suggests fine wine in exquisite crystal. Mariel extracts the essence, layers it with subtlety, and sets it down straight

into your heart. Her ability to inhabit the lyric, to make it her own, is heard on every track.... And the simplistic elegance of 'But Beautiful' is the perfect opener to set the mood."

—Judith Pine Bobe, Founder/Director
Heart of Carolina Jazz Society

And there I was: on stage. And just like with my album, I opened with "But Beautiful."

I had become a strawberry blonde for the event. Joe liked it. He was out there, somewhere in the crowd. If you've ever been on stage, you know how hard it is to see everyone since the lights are so bright. Fortunately, you don't need to see *everyone*. All you need to do is sing to one person. Joe was my person. He was lost in the crowd, making them think I was singing just for them.

Performing to a "standing room only" at Chico's House of Jazz...hearing the quiet between my lyrics and the riot at songs' end...remembering the girl with the soup ladle on the red vinyl chair in Park Slope, Brooklyn...knowing how hard she had worked to stand on this bigger stage now...this was ecstasy.

I was simply swept away when my friends and family approached me with praise at the end of the show—I was taken to a place I had never been. I was "enjoying the journey," as they say. Well, reaching the destination is where it's at, if you ask me. The feeling was incredible. I knew at that moment that I was a jazz artist—that I had something different and special. Now, how to make a living at it was a different story! But tonight I had the package; I sang the songs, had affected the audience, was wearing *the* dress, had a debut album entitled *Mariel Larsen*, and was blessed by the love of a good man. It was January 29, 2012. I wasn't twenty-one, or even thirty-one, but it no longer mattered. I had arrived.

Two days later, Dustin was dead.

Just like that, my light, my sunrise, my rapture had snapped to black.

My only child was gone.

two

Joe

LIFE WAS GOOD. HELL, MY life was always good. Even as a kid, even when my parents got divorced when I was nine, life was still *okay*. I mean, it changed everything, but it's not like I sat around and pouted over my oatmeal about it. I was busy playing ball, chasing the neighborhood girls, and watching sports and the evening news. I was especially interested in science and technology. My mother thought I was bonding with my father when I put down the baseball mitt and focused on the evening news. Trust me, I wasn't. I was interested in science, business, money, and how it all worked.

I didn't last long at home. By eighteen, I was out, and roomed with friends until I saved enough money to get my own place. My parents sent me to a parochial grammar school and high school, encouraging me to follow in my father's medical footsteps. That didn't work out too well. I was asked to leave college during my freshman year in pre-med for organizing card games in between classes. Hey, science came easy to me—I got bored! After that I realized being a doctor wasn't for me. I imagined myself selling medical equipment on the black market or something. So I turned my educational focus 180 degrees and took up business as my new major. I was accepted into a university known as "Harvard on the Hackensack" and graduated with a BS in Business Management. I started, and eventually sold, many businesses but my favorite was LifeSavers Limousine. I got married during this period, too. And there wasn't anything wrong with that, except that we wanted different things. She wanted me to be a father, a real family man. I enjoyed being with someone, having love, but I wasn't ready for a family. When I was a kid, my family disappeared. After that, I had friends. They never disappeared.

Anyway, I loved life as a business owner, and New York City made for one heck of a playground. If my limo company wasn't driving an out-of-towner to a big business meeting at the Ritz, we were caravanning around to the Village or the Garden to see Zepplin, ELP, YES, and Dylan. And when that wasn't happening, we were kicking it up at the afterhours clubs until four a.m. But I always made it home by the time the sun rose...and back to the office by seven. My career was the world to me.

One night in the spring of 1985, I was wrapping up paperwork when out of nowhere appeared this beautiful woman named Lisa. She bounced in selling space in the Yellow Pages. She had talent, which she used to try talking me into increasing my advertising. I talked her into closing the deal over a couple dirty martinis, or at least that's what I thought at the time. We were to meet the following evening.

The Following Evening

It was almost seven when Lisa arrived, but she wasn't alone. She brought along a real showstopper from head to toe. I could tell she was feisty the second we made eye contact. She was slender but curvy, sophisticated, and wearing a suit that looked tailor-made. It showed off her legs and made me think she held majority stock in Bell all at the same time. That was some suit. I was all ears, all eyes, and shoved both hands in my pockets because when in doubt, that's the best place for 'em.

MaryAnn Larsen. She was the closer. Lisa thought she needed backup, and brought the big gun! Boy, did it work. I not only renewed my contracts but they bumped me up threefold—to three thousand dollars per month. That was a chunk back then.

Thank God she didn't ask for more advertising. I would have signed over my IRA.

I didn't get a martini out of the deal that day, but as time passed I received so much more.

Nine years later, MaryAnn and I were married. That was twenty-two years ago and I have never stopped loving her.

It's not my job to understand why bad things happen to decent people. I've always believed in the Higher Power, and since marrying the love of my life, it's made my faith even stronger. Her father, mother, and son, Dustin, became my family. Her dad was like a father to me, and her mom, Theresa, was a saint who joined our Heavenly Father after succumbing to a bout with lung cancer six months after our 1994 wedding. Theresa knew about her diagnosis at the wedding but saved us the heartbreak. That's the kind of mother MaryAnn had. I knew Dustin when he was sixteen years old. God, I loved that kid. He loved surfing  and filmmaking and made it his goal to surf the big waves and film the experience. And he did it. He was a go-getter like MaryAnn. It was in the genes.

Aside from MaryAnn not having the kind of career success she had been striving for, we had it good. After the sale of my limousine company, I started a Telecommunication company, reselling and re-billing long distance services. That was during the time of the Bell breakups. Business was great! I sold the business to a publically traded company and put a few pennies away before starting an Internet ISP and web development company in 1994. That's when it was reported that Al Gore created the Internet. He was the first political leader to recognize the importance of the Internet and to promote and support its development. I took that information and ran with it.

In 1998, I merged with WebMaster USA, another web design and infrastructure company. We were ready to launch our IPO, which would have made us a tremendous amount of cash, when the technology bubble burst in 2000. So I dusted myself off and founded Titan-MMS, another technology company specializing in computer networking and software applications. I designed an online LOS (loan origination software). My chief software engineer was Allen Pollack, an exceptional coder. This drew me into the Real Estate Investment and finance world. At the time, it saved me.

I was thriving in real estate and mortgage financing. And, of course, I was continuing to dabble in new endeavors—one of which was executive producing a twenty-minute animated short called *Once Upon a Christmas Village*. This was supposed to be the teaser for the full feature film. It was directed by a very talented person and friend, Michael Attardi and starred the voiceovers of Jim Belushi, Tim Curry, and Amanda Davis. I raised the money and we spent a year in production. Then we toured the globe, winning over six dozen awards, including Cannes in 2007 as First Runner Up for Short Animation. At one time, this short held the world record for wins.

MaryAnn couldn't travel with me for most of it. It wasn't in the budget. Plus, she had her career and nine-to-five job to think about. I flew her out for the last festival in Annecy, France, though. What a beautiful city.

Then we returned home. That was when the housing market crashed and took the entire economy with it.

I was scrambling to save us from sinking into the economic tidal wave that inundated so many other Americans. They say that you should be ready with six months' worth of savings; I had eighteen. I was prepared.

It wasn't enough.

MaryAnn has never been involved in our finances. She's worked fulltime since the day I met her but I've always been the pro in that department. I liked having control over it. The market crash took that control away. For MaryAnn, the money had always come in. For me, the guy behind the scenes, I knew it would be a long time before I could sleep through the night again. We blew through eighteen months of savings and nearly lost our home. By 2009, I was seeking a primary mortgage modification and sold all investment properties to save us.

It worked.

In 2010, I opened a retail mortgage office specializing in home mortgages. After four years of economic turmoil, we were back on track.

This brings me to January 29, 2012. We were at Chico's House of Jazz for the first of many performances scheduled to promote MaryAnn's CD, *Mariel Larsen* (her stage name). I was so proud of her. She looked the part. She had arrived. And her voice left me speechless. Hearing her sing was like listening to angels, except it was such a turn on. By that I mean that when MaryAnn sings, anyone within earshot is transfixed at a fundamental level.

Money is the number one reason people get divorced. We survived that test. I couldn't breathe for four years. After taking in the sight and sounds of my beautiful wife at Chico's, I finally exhaled.

As I said, I'm not the guy who questions "why." I find solutions and answers; *I'm that guy*. But what's the solution when your wife's only child takes his own life? How do I fix that? We had just recovered from near economic ruin. MaryAnn had worked a lifetime to gain recognition in her field as a jazz singer.

We worked so hard.

She worked so hard.

On February 1, 2012, it all vanished along with Dustin's death.

three

MaryAnn

IN MID-JANUARY OF 2012, THREE weeks before Dustin's death, I had taken him to the Albert Ellis Institute, a world-renowned psychotherapy-training institute for an evaluation.

I knew something was up. A mother knows. He was my only son and I could feel his ongoing pain. This doesn't mean that I was prepared to deal with his suicide. This means that my child needed help for a very long time.

He used to call me in the middle of the night.

"Mom, I don't feel well."

I'd ask, "Do you have a fever? Did you take your temperature? Do you have a stomachache? What can I do, Dustin?"

His answer was always, "No, it's not that...." He was vague. I was a fool to think that maybe he just wanted to hear me. The sound of my voice would make it all better.

He called the night before he died. I asked all the questions a mom naturally would. I wanted to get out of bed and drive to his home in Oakland but I had a breakfast meeting with my manager the next day. It seemed irrational, too. And we were waiting on the results from Albert Ellis, which was a step in the right direction. I kept telling myself that the results, no matter what they are, would ease some of his pain. I assumed Dustin thought like that too, and that he was also looking forward to the results. I reassured him we'd chat in the morning and went back to sleep.

My cell phone started playing Ireland's National Anthem. This was the ringtone I had programmed for my dad.

As my manager paid the bill for breakfast, I literally said out loud, "He's up early!" It was only half past eight.

I picked up and barely got in a *hello* when my dad said, "I have bad news, MaryAnn."

"Okay. Did the furnace blow up?"

He was quiet for a bit, then said, "Dustin committed suicide."

"You're scaring me, Dad." I thought he was joking. Not an actual joke; the words just didn't make sense. I couldn't believe it since I had just spoken to him the previous night. Plus, I was calling him in ten minutes, as we had planned. My manager was paying the tab, the breakfast meeting was over, and I was going to call Dustin like I had promised. In ten minutes. I kept my word with my son, with everyone. He was expecting my call. How could he take his own life when he was expecting my call? It didn't make sense.

Hysteria doesn't take long to settle in. Even if the mind can't keep up, all sorts of reflexes kick in—shaking, sweating, racing heart. My voice echoed throughout the restaurant. I had no control over any of it. I started saying "*Oh, my God, Oh, my God,*" over and over. "Check to see if he's breathing, Dad. You need to go back and check. He's sleeping, Dad. Go check. Go—"

"He's gone, MaryAnn. He's gone. The police are here. The police are already here." My Dad repeated himself.

I've played this conversation over in my head a trillion times since Dustin's death. I have it down, word for word. Sometimes it plays a trillion times in just one day. Dad kept saying everything twice—a habit he had when he wanted to emphasize that something was really, really true.

"Call the ambulance, Dad! You need to call an ambulance! Right now!" No matter what he said, I kept at it.

There's no way to prepare for a call like that.

Back in 2004, when finances were tight, Dad had suggested Dustin move in with him. So he did. My son was living in my old psychedelic downstairs bedroom in Oakland, New Jersey. Dad was such a caring man. He said, "I'm investing in his future. Just think of all the money he'll save now that he's rent-free." And Dustin was able to launch Liquid Illusion, a website promoting his own creative endeavors. He did freelance website design, too. He had collaborated with renowned photographer Kendall Messick to design his website and focus on photography. He took the most revealing and thought-provoking photo of my father I have ever seen, which was used in Kendall's American Life series, highlighting the elderly. But Dad and I knew it wasn't just about the money. He, too, worried about how Dustin always seemed to feel sick when nothing on the surface appeared to be wrong.

Again, in 2008, when Dustin was extra depressed because he was going through a divorce, his room was waiting for him at Dad's. Joe and I were relieved he was back there. My dad was a father, grandfather, and lifelong mentor to Dustin.

I discovered later that morning that Dad found him hanging in the walk-in wardrobe.

I can't imagine.

A month later, I received a bill in the mail from the Albert Ellis Institute. It said if I was interested in the full evaluation report on Dustin, I would need to pay the balance and they would mail it. I called them immediately and reported the news. They wanted to see me and said that they would release the report at no cost. Dr. Albert Ellis, who died in 2007, was considered one of the greatest living psychotherapists. His colleagues compared him to Sigmund Freud.

I sure as hell wanted to know what the Albert Ellis Institute had to say about Dustin.

They discovered he had a very rare mental illness called Body Dysmorphic Disorder.

A person with this disorder becomes obsessed with defects in their appearance. For example, a slight difference in the shape of the eyes or an ear that is slightly higher than the other can drive a person with this disorder into madness. We all have this. Nobody's perfect. God made us all unique but I couldn't convince my sweet son of that. BDD is similar to anorexia in that the sufferer has unattainable and unhealthy standards. Deep self-loathing drives every thought. BDD affects men and women equally, comprising between one and two percent of the population. Suicide is a major side effect. Body Dysmorphic Disorder is often diagnosed post-mortem. It is very much a social anxiety disorder.

How do you convince a perfectly beautiful person they are perfect and beautiful when they don't feel it?

Dustin was an artist, photographer, and filmmaker. He was a deep thinker like many artists. Creativity can come from anywhere when your right brain is in the driver's seat. A shredded garbage bag in a New York City alleyway can look like art if the breeze is ruffling it while the light is hitting it just so. Dustin's brow was often wrinkled in the center of his forehead, indicating that he was figuring something out—how to color the world with his vision. He was stopped cold, daily, by the wonders around him He was the kid who saw into the soul of the earth and found profound beauty in a discarded plastic bag. But when I'd tell him he was my perfect handsome boy, his brow would relax. It wasn't peace that bathed over him. He'd go blank, confused by my nonsense. It wouldn't compute.

The first time I noticed this was when he was seven. We were in my car waiting for the soccer coach to get organized and call the players onto the field. When the whistle blew and I said, "Let's go, sweetie," he just sat there. He wouldn't budge or unbuckle his seatbelt. I noticed he was looking at what he was wearing. Perhaps he was thinking about how his shorts or shirt had a wrinkle in them or his socks weren't white enough. He didn't want any of his friends to see him that way. He was always concerned about how he looked. He didn't want to be embarrassed.

He was just as self-conscious when he went to high school years later at the elite Don Bosco Prep in Ramsey, New Jersey. He'd spend hours in the bathroom in the morning with the lights out. As a mother I should have realized that wasn't normal. I'd yell, "Please turn the light on! How can you see your face?" I had no idea that my gorgeous son, blessed with crystal blue eyes and high cheekbones, was dying of embarrassment. It was the start of the dysmorphia.

Was I still a mom? Was I? He was my one and only. Beyond that riddle, which remains, was I a singer? A wife? A daughter? I wonder if anything even mattered anymore. People would ask about the album. I'd have to fake it and pretend that sales mattered. Or smile and be grateful that they liked my voice and my music enough to inquire. I wasn't glad about it. I was pissed off at everybody and life in general. Except Joe. He got me. He let the sadness pool about the house. He didn't attempt to mop any of it up. He let me simply be me.

Dustin was the main reason I had faith in the process. He was why "waiting another day" was A-okay. I had him. Fame would come. A singing career was all I've ever wanted, but it was still secondary to being his mom.

I'm not suggesting that our relationship was without flaws. Our children work us and wear us down. It was exhausting managing Dustin sometimes. I had hoped his marriage would have fixed most of what was wrong but now I can see that that was naïve of me. Marriage doesn't fix problems, not the first time around anyway, not in my experience.

Reviews kept coming in about my show at Chico's. People were asking what was next for me. I couldn't escape the thought that none of it mattered. I was five seconds from crying every waking minute of my life without Dustin. How could I get through another show? I couldn't get through a vocal lesson, a load of laundry, or even a cup of coffee without tears materializing. The stage? Suddenly that was my past. My destiny took on the significance of the weather report. People asked, but it didn't change anything....

This was February 2012.

I watched his short films and looked at his photographs. I was framing them in duplicate and triplicate in an attempt to get back my past, to be Dustin's mom again.

I was not looking forward to March, other than, maybe, just maybe, to get a good night's sleep. Maybe my brain would need a break by then, and I'd sleep through the night. Maybe I would quit blaming myself for not driving to my dad's house in Oakland at midnight on Tuesday, January 31, 2012. Maybe I would take a break from the hate. I just wanted a nap, that's all. I guess I thought that March, the dawn of spring, would bring a nap.

I was keeping my wishes small and simple.

DUSTIN KERSNOWSKI

September 29, 1973 ~ February 1, 2012

four

J o e

BY THE TIME I WENT on a first date with MaryAnn, we had known each other for a long time—nearly a dozen years. She wanted to cook dinner for me at her place. Dustin was sixteen at the time. MaryAnn didn't ask what my preferences were, and I didn't tell her, although I would've put money on it being Italian.

I didn't know I was going to meet Dustin that night but I'm a fan of spontaneity. MaryAnn was clearly comfortable enough to have her son present on a date, which made me feel good inside. She had candles lit, Nat King Cole on the stereo, a sweet kid who was easy to be around, and a nice bottle of red. This date was perfect right up until she served the stuffed flounder. I thought something smelled fishy. I'm more of a steak guy. That being said, I could've pulled through had it been almost any other fish. But I was being served seafood stuffed with more seafood. It was overkill, if you know what I mean. I moved my food around the plate as long as I could. Thankfully, MaryAnn got up to go to the bathroom. It was just Dustin and me and that plate of flounder. I didn't have the heart to tell MaryAnn how I felt since she had gone through all the trouble. But I didn't have the stomach to suffer any longer, either. Meanwhile, the kid was sitting across from me eating a pizza. I picked up my plate, slid the stuffed flounder into the trash, did some quick rearranging, and sat back down. Dustin didn't say a word, God bless him, but he was looking at me kind of funny so I pulled out my wallet, handed him a five, and said, "It'd be great if this was just between us."

He grinned and offered me a slice of the pie. I took two and inhaled those before MaryAnn returned.

We were tight after that, Dustin and me. We shared a moment, as they say.

I believe I was the happiest I had ever been that night MaryAnn sang at Chico's House of Jazz. I've had many moments of bliss like that with her—that fun first date, our two weddings. That night at Chico's was one of them, too. And then, two days later, I was as destroyed as I'd ever been by Dustin's death. I thought my parents getting divorced was bad. I was just a kid. MaryAnn's sweet mother dying of cancer was heartbreaking as hell. The housing bubble leveled us financially, and that was terrifying. The stress was intense. Sinking for two years and taking MaryAnn down with me, feeling responsible yet victimized by a force bigger than myself, and not having anyone to talk to about it with was tough. But losing a child tragically and without warning is the worst thing in the world. You don't know the meaning of the word helpless until you or someone you love loses a child. We've never fought over who loved him more. MaryAnn gave birth to him. But I loved my son so much. I had to both grieve and hold up the rest of my world, which was MaryAnn, so she could let go.

Things didn't get easier with time. But the letter from the Albert Ellis Institute, which came near the end of February, brought a small measure of relief. It brought answers. We're both proactive people. That letter prompted us to launch The Bungalow Foundation (TheBungalow.org), a 501(c)(3) nonprofit dedicated to assisting artists suffering from mental disorders. It later expanded into a much larger organization, including cancer research funding.

MaryAnn had something to focus on, which gave me some relief.

One day when I was working from home shortly after The Bungalow was up and running, I heard her practicing her *do-re-mi's*. It was the first time I had smiled all month. I don't think anyone gets over this sort of thing, but hope was surfacing.

MaryAnn's father was a real trooper. I have a lot of respect for that guy. Artie got MaryAnn out of the house. Finally. Back when our son was still alive, we had our favorite restaurants, songs, holidays, and shoes, just like the rest of the world. Well, Artie and MaryAnn ventured out for the first time in weeks to her favorite café, the Bagel Hut. I don't know how it felt to be out in the world; I wasn't with them. Maybe they were stuck staring at each other, not knowing how to act or what to say, stuck talking about the weather. At least it was sunny. Spring was peeking into the Eastern sky. It was March 5, 2012. MaryAnn didn't wake up crying once last night. It was only Monday. Still, it made me think: *this week is going to be a little bit better.*

I was at work when I got the call.

MaryAnn and Artie were leaving the Bagel Hut, making their way out of the parking lot to turn into traffic when an older gentlemen in a 1992 Toyota SUV jumped the curb at forty-five miles an hour. He hit the driver's side dead on, crashing into MaryAnn. The Jaws of Life had to remove my beautiful wife from the car after the entire roof was sawed off. The driver's seat had been crushed. The impact had moved it over twenty-two inches. A helicopter landed shortly thereafter to fly MaryAnn to Robert Wood Johnson University Hospital, where a level 1 trauma team was waiting to save her life or at least try the best they could.

Artie was banged up, too, but he was going to live. Thank God for that.

But my MaryAnn didn't do as well. She had two collapsed lungs, a lacerated liver and gallbladder, and a shattered pelvis. All of her ribs, each one of them, were broken and she had two lacerated carotid arteries. Her blood pressure was extremely low. They had to give her several blood transfusions over the next couple days just to keep her alive. Then they induced a coma to reduce the stress on her body. She'd spent March in a coma. How ironic, I heard her praying for sleep just a few nights back. She thought it might bring her peace—to sleep through the night.

After everything that had happened, I now had to deal with this.

If my wife pulled through and somehow miraculously fully recovered. Perhaps I could look back and say she needed a break from life. I could conclude that that was the purpose of the car accident. But I was far from being capable of that kind of spiritual assessment.

I could no longer go into work. Not at all. February was hit and miss as it was, but for March, I closed the book on going into the office completely. I sat by her side and talked and read to her. MaryAnn learned more about golf than she ever wanted to know. If I didn't have the golf channel on, I was reading to her. I read *How to Play Golf 101*, cover to cover. Was I supposed to read something she'd be into? I didn't have a manual for this. No one had written *How to Deal with Tragedy on Top of Tragedy for Dummies* yet.

Even though I could no longer work under this kind of stress, the laptop kept me connected to The Bungalow Foundation and

Facebook. In spite of everything, I was thankful for technology and good friends, every day.

Joe Anselmo

March 6, 2012

Maryann update—

She is in an induced coma. She is still losing blood (2 more units during the night). But she's in the best hospital for treatment. Robert Wood Johnson University Hospital (RWJ) in New Brunswick is the only level 1 trauma hospital in New Jersey. Will keep everyone posted. Sorry No Visitors Allowed at this time.

I am sorry that we haven't had a lot of posts lately, and I'm hoping everyone is doing well. I wanted to announce the co-founder of The Bungalow, Dustin's mom and grandfather, were involved in a horrific car accident on Monday. I am sorry that I can't respond to all of your well wishes, as I am totally overwhelmed. Please keep Dustin in your prayers and pray for MaryAnn and her dad's speedy recovery. Thanks, Joseph Anselmo

March 7, 2012

I cannot thank you enough for your support and prayers. Thank you all. MaryAnn was sedated during the night and was made as comfortable as possible. She took on one additional unit of blood which is down from yesterday's two. They tell me her body is equalizing. Equalizing? Okay, I guess they know best; why would they keep anything from me? In three days she's taken 21 units. All other vital signs are strong so that's good news. I've got my laptop with me now so I'll be sending "good news" updates live.

P.S. there's no confirmation yet from the 72-year-old who jumped the curb and crashed into her. They say it was a medical episode. Please say a prayer for him, as he must be going through some pretty heavy mental conflicts. Let's also advocate driver retesting at certain ages if for nothing else reflects and reactions.

March 8, 2012

Sorry, there is no change; her hemoglobin count is still low (7) and so 2 more units of hemoglobin today (plus one last night), plus 1 unit of platelets. Vitals signs are still very strong, thank God.

I'm so saddened that I can't help her, protect her from the pain, and be inside her heart—be with her. All I can do is hold her hand and talk. ...Then I put CNBC on for a little while. Maybe she'll become an expert in doing her finances. Lol

Dad's better...he was up and in a chair for the first time. Tomorrow he's being moved to a rehab facility. There's still no visitors, but cards are welcome. I'll read every single one to her.

March 9, 2012

No blood today, and they removed the drainage tubes from her right lung. Good girl! She's strong! It's got to be the Italian in her.

She does, however, have a small fever. They will determine over the next few days from culture samples where it is, and what to fight (fingers and toes crossed). Unfortunately she was not awake today. I had the golf channel on most of the day, hopefully she'll get interested in the game. Not!

Blood pressure was low due to the fever but all other vitals were still strong. Sorry this is coming to you so late but it was a long day and I came home to a surprise dinner with family, which is always a good thing. No matter what, turn to family and friends when in doubt. They will always be there for you!

March 10, 2012

She had a quiet night still with fever but not as high and no more blood. Yeah!!! They are performing a bronchoscopy in a little while. With this procedure they can see abnormalities and foreign bodies, and what's going on in her lungs. They will also take mucus samples to test for bacteria so they can treat with the specific antibiotic.

March 11, 2012

MaryAnn, still heavily sedated, was comfortable last night. Her blood culture revealed the nasty Gram Negative Rod bacteria. I will know more later when her doctors come in. The question is where exactly is it and what type of debridement will they recommend?

Her fever was 103 yesterday morning, and down to 99 last night when I left. This morning it's back up to 100.3. Her right groin is still draining; her left lung is still draining; she still has that damn hematoma in her bladder; embolism in her carotid artery; still on a respirator, and still in critical but stable condition. What does that mean exactly? How can someone have so many new issues but still be stable?

Today is Sunday, the seventh day of this nightmare. Where are you, Mare? Please come back to me. I can't live without you. This is so difficult—for me to see you like this every day and every night. I miss your singing, your smile, your touch, even your stupid jokes. Please come back to me right now. Stop fooling around and get out of that damn bed…!

March 12, 2012

MaryAnn's condition is still critical—the good news is they removed the drainage tubes from her left lung, good girl! The bad news is she now has pneumonia.

I know it's very difficult for some of you to read these posts every day, but please hang in there; she's a strong girl with a tremendous amount of will to live. My strength comes from your daily posts. I'm sorry I can't answer everyone, but I really appreciate your well wishes and prayers for Mare. If any of you need to talk with someone or just sound off, don't forget about www.theBungalow.org. There are people there, including mental health professionals that may help.

32

March 12, 2012 (later that night)

MaryAnn's condition is still critical BUT at around 1:45 p.m. she opened her eyes and was checking out the room, and she responded to a few toe wiggling commands. She was aware and that's all that counts. I read her a few of your cards, which put a smile on her face. Please keep those prayers coming in. It's working!

She's not out of the woods yet, but she's fighting! The hematoma in her bladder is subsiding and she still has that abscess in her carotid artery, but for now they are concentrating on treating her pneumonia.

I am hopeful that she will be fully aware by tomorrow. She is still on the respirator but her doctors say she may be off by Thursday. Thank you all for your prayers, the prayers from the Vatican, and the masses that have been said in her name. One has to believe that all you need is a flicker of life to save someone. Never give up, always be there, and let faith guide you. As my dear friend Richard Nanes always said, "Thank you, and goodbye for now."

March 13, 2012

MaryAnn is still fighting for her life. Eight days ago when she was first admitted the doctors told me she would take two steps forward and one backward then two more steps forward and one backward again. Today she took two steps backward. They didn't prepare me for that part.

She's fighting two infections, her fever was 103 most of the day and her heart rate was very high. She wasn't too aware of anything in that condition but what worries me most is she can't move her hands or arms on command. Moving her toes and feet are no problem. She's going in for another cat scan tonight. Sorry, I wish I had better news.

March 14, 2012

Freehold Group—John, Wendy and everyone: thank you for all your support. I am confident that our belief in God and your prayers will guide her through this nightmare. She is an incredible woman—a jazz singer. Did you know that? Here's a picture of her from her website that our son Dustin started (a work in progress). http://www.mariellarsen.com Mariel is her stage name. Her last sold out show was at Chico's House of Jazz in Asbury Park. I'll be bringing in her iPod today. Hopefully she'll respond to her favorite music.

March 14, 2012

Sorry, I don't know what to write. The CAT scan revealed multiple strokes. I'll know more later tonight after they review her EEG. She's responding to me as though I'm one of her doctors, with disinterest. I'm losing my honey, my baby, my best friend and I can't do a damn thing about it. I will never give up as long as there's a glimmer of life in her. She is such a talented singer/songwriter; I just want to see her on stage again.

If there's someone out there in state government please advocate legislation to retest drivers on "reaction time" when reaching a certain age.

Goodnight and God Bless.

March 15, 2012

MaryAnn's condition is critical but stable. I cannot go into detail regarding her treatment. I've been instructed to keep all future updates to a few words. Sorry.

March 19, 2012

Day 14—still critical but stable

I told the Powers that Be that I need to give a quick update so here goes: MaryAnn was extubated Sunday afternoon at 12:30 p.m., but by 5:30 a.m. she could not continue to breathe on her own. She was completely exhausted and had to be put on a BiPAP respiration system and sedated. Visitors are not permitted until she has enough strength to breathe on her own. She continues to fight and her body continues to repair itself.

March 22, 2012

Day 17 in SICU

MaryAnn's recovery is short of a miracle. Keep those prayers coming! She has successfully been weaned off the BiPAP respirator but still has a great deal of fluids to pass. She's still on antibiotics, Haprin, and fluids, but it seems as though the worst is behind her. She's still on a feeding tube, and she cannot speak or swallow foods due to her inflamed throat and vocal chords. We do not know the permanent extent of damage the 3 strokes have caused but the doctors are hopeful.

She was moved out of SICU at 5:30 p.m. I am broadcasting to you live from our new home in the Tower Building at RWJ Hospital. Her new mailing address has changed to room T947. Bye for now.

March 23, 2012

Day 18 in SICU

It's really tough writing these posts.... MaryAnn only lasted eight hours on the floor before being sent back to the Special Intensive Care Unit. She had to be re-intubated at 2:00 a.m. "No Visitors Allowed" at this time. Your prayers are being heard, it's just such a long process. Not many people would have survived that horrific crash.

March 28, 2012

Day 23 in SICU

MaryAnn is still in SICU but her condition is improving. Yesterday (Tuesday), we sat her in a chair for the first time. She still has a pneumodart in her right chest cavity treating the pneumothorax in her right lung. She's still on a feeding tube. One of her stokes affected her ability to swallow. Rehab and time will bring that back to normal. Her balder Foley was removed last night. She will be on blood thinners for a long time to reduce the risk of additional strokes. She's tired and aggravated and wants to come home. She cannot talk, but I read her very well. I am grateful she's getting stronger every day, and hopeful that she'll recover to one hundred percent. You cannot believe how your prayers and support have helped me through this ordeal, and MaryAnn, too. Thank you and bye for now.

April 2, 2012

Week 5 in SICU

At the request of MaryAnn's psychiatrist there are "No Visitors Allowed." She cannot assimilate multiple conversations and what appears normal to us is very confusing to her, which makes her anxious and slows her recovery. MaryAnn's condition is good one day and bad the next. Her left vocal cord is still paralyzed, so she cannot speak (or swallow—dysphagia—has a nasal tube for her feeding). Her right lung cavity is filling with liquid so she's having another procedure this afternoon to insert a chest tube into the area for drainage. Her increased heartbeat has not slowed, so she's still on beta blockers, and other meds including, Haprin, to fight other symptoms. Tomorrow a decision will be made to remove whether to remove the nasogastric tube and substitute it with gastrostomy tube (G-tube) directly into the stomach. And just when you think things are getting better. Well, that's my update.

April 12, 2012

I know it been a long time coming and everyone's anxious to hear about MaryAnn's condition. Well, she's not back on water skis but she is out of ICU and Robert Wood Johnson's Hospital. I had her moved to JFK Medical Center in Edison. She's in the brain trauma unit of their rehab center. She's still pretty badly banged up, has paralyzed vocal chords, can't swallow, and has a G-tube in her stomach for feeding. But she's fighting with all of her doctors and therapists so I guess that's a good thing. Visiting hours are from 4:30 p.m. to 8:00 p.m. Monday – Friday in the Brain trauma unit and from 1:00 to 8:00 p.m. weekends. DO NOT GIVE HER WATER OR ANYTHING TO DRINK OR EAT! SHE WILL ASK YOU SO BE AWARE.

April 23, 2012

Week 9

MaryAnn's in great spirits and is anxious for the day she comes home. She passed her speech and swallowing test this morning and is now allowed to eat regular food. Hopefully, the G-tube comes out in a few days. She continues to battle other challenges but she's getting there.

May 1, 2012

Week 10

MaryAnn's improvement in rehab is so progressive that we decided to continue rehabilitation from home. Dad, who came home a few days ago, continues his rehabilitation from home as well. YIPPEE! Let the wheelchair races begin! All kidding aside, I want to:

—Thank God that both Dad and MaryAnn are healing toward a full recovery.
—Thank all of you for your prayers and that this day has finally come.
—Thank every person for your words of support, email, Facebook, text messages, phone calls, and over 300 "Get Well" cards that were received.
—Thank the volunteers for the work and services you have generously organized.

I am finally back to work full time (after three seemingly endless months), and would like to give to every one of you whatever I can from my business and the banking services that I offer. In appreciation of whatever business you can give to me, (and believe me, I certainly need it now more than anything else), I'll start the offer off with waived application fees and appraisal fees to you, your family, friends, and/or clients if you would refer me for residential or commercial financing.

Tonight I'm planning on saying one big prayer thanking all of you.

Thank you!

five

MaryAnn

IT HAPPENED INSTANTANEOUSLY UPON IMPACT. One second I was leaving the Bagel Hut, Dad was fiddling with my CD, trying to put it in the player, longing to hear his little girl sing again. Then suddenly everything went white.

I was spared the physical pain of feeling my ribs and pelvis shatter due to the impact of being T-boned directly into my driver's side door. You can't breathe very well when a rib cracks. All of mine were broken, as I was later told. I didn't feel a thing.

Dad and I didn't talk about the weather at Bagel Hut. Music was the topic of the morning over Taylor ham & egg sandwiches. It was just a veil, though. We were both thinking about Dustin. I imagine Dad was wondering what he did wrong like I was. I never thought to ask him that, though.

I got pregnant with Dustin at the age of seventeen. I was a child myself. My mother and father loved, supported, and assisted me, like second and third parents in the raising of my son. A person goes through all kinds of adversity bringing a child into the world while they're so young and unprepared. My parents were gifts from God. In that way, Dad had lost a son, too. His main concern was my well-being, though. And he was so proud we were out of the house. I could see the worry in his eyes but it was mixed with hope so I kept a brave face throughout breakfast. I didn't cry once. It wasn't easy but I told myself that for one full hour, I could fake a few smiles and make small talk with my beautiful father. That way, I'd earn the right to cry when I got back to the safety of my home. I was so close to that kind of freedom, the kind where it doesn't matter what you wear, or what you say, or how often you cry; you are still loved. Home was minutes away. Freedom was just a drive home. And it wasn't even rush hour. I had made it through a meal in public. I had earned the right to collapse onto my bed and cry until Joe's arms found me that evening.

We paid the tab, shared a friendly goodbye with the staff, and hopped into the Jeep. Dad got into the passenger's side. We shared the smallest of victory smiles for having ventured out. He knew how hard that was. I backed out and drove to where the parking lot met Route 34.

That's where everything went white.

It was as if a heavy fog came down and engulfed the vehicle. I jerked my head in every direction searching for Joe, my rock. That's when some of the fog thinned. I was surrounded by shattered glass in every direction. In another instant, I was swept above the rubble. I had been carried away.

That's when Dustin appeared.

He was so handsome in his button-down and linen slacks. He wasn't the kind of guy who wore button-downs regularly, and I found that odd, but he was right in front of me for the first time in weeks. I had so much to say and I didn't know where to begin, but I surely wasn't going to start with, "What's up with your shirt?" I had little interest in his attire.

It felt like he saved me from something, as I was suddenly injected with a sense of peace I hadn't felt since his death. This peace syphoned its way into my bones. It was ecstasy in the spiritual sense of the word. Dustin finally spoke. He said he was lost, though he didn't seem scared. I told him that was impossible. I was standing right here. "I'm your home, Dustin," I responded. But as I looked around, I realized what he meant.

Even though I couldn't tell you whether we were outside or in, I will say it was the clearest of days and the fog was a distant memory. The temperature was perfect, I guess. I couldn't feel a breeze but I wasn't hot. My dress didn't make much sense, either.

As I looked down upon this scene of me with my son, as if I had a bird's eye view of it all, I was wearing a white dress that was a bit frilly. I didn't do white or frilly, but never mind about that either.

He said it again, "I think I'm lost."

"Well, take my hand, dear."

He was standing a whole room away but he grabbed my hand easily.

"I'm sorry our last breakfast together was cut short. I'm so—"

"Don't be silly, Mom."

I was terribly guilt-ridden over leaving our last breakfast date early. I had added a few Peggy Lee numbers to the Chico's lineup in the final week before show time. This shouldn't have been a problem, except that the original pianist had to cancel for a Norah Jones/Katherine McPhee booking at the last minute. It's understandable now but at the time I was angry. I blamed him and a few others for bailing, which caused the last-minute shift in my opening night's arrangement and required me to rehearse overtime and cut into the last meal I would ever have with my son. I've blamed the hell out of my band members since Dustin has passed. There was too much pain, anger, guilt, and grief to keep it all contained. It had to go somewhere. So I directed it at my band—the people that had worked tirelessly to make sure the big night at Chico's House of Jazz had the impact we all knew it could.

"Mom, I'm so glad you came."

"Where else would I go, Dustin? Where else?"

We chatted for a long, long while, my favorite son and I. I think he believed me for the first time when I told him God had crafted him to perfection. He was tall. His crystal blue eyes and high cheekbones were things of envy; his hair was thick and silky, not unlike my own. We were both artistic, and good hair was in the genes, too. He didn't need the "enhancements," the procedure he had recently endured, that was for sure. He was an attractive boy who grew into a handsome, distinguished man. Growing up, and well into his adult life, I had always thought he was shy, a personality trait that seemed to attract women. I was so saddened by the fact that I had failed to notice the problem beyond the symptoms. It was so "western" of me.

It seemed as if he believed me for the first time ever, here in this place that was neither outside nor in, neither hot nor cold, day nor night. He believed me when I told him that he was beautiful and smiled easily. It was clear that he wanted peace but didn't know how to get it.

When you say you love me,
Why do I feel that it's a lie?

I wrote the lyrics to "When You Say You Love Me" thinking it was just another love song, intending it to be. At the time, I was recording with Grammy award-winning music publishers Richard Joseph and Mia Rebel, who were at the top of their game crafting and selling platinum hits to superstars like Celine Dion. That song was going on the album, along with "Through Fire and Rain," co-written by Richard, Mia, and myself. I was trying to be profound with these songs, write hits; they were going to be it. Little did I know the impact these studio sessions would one day have on my heart. These weren't lyrics for love of my life, Joe, as intended. Hidden inside the lines of these songs were messages to my future self. "When You Say You Love Me" was a love letter from my beloved child. It was written to help me understand him, so that I might one day heal from events that were yet to occur. "Through Fire and Rain" foretold of my battle with loss and cancer. This was the first of many opportunities for which I allowed myself to bend the rules of reality and dissect "Through Fire and Rain," my first writing endeavor, any my other music, too.

We walked for hours, maybe days, hand in hand. I don't know how I knew the path to heaven. As far as I knew, I'd never been. But there we were, travelling the road together. My son was lost and he sought my assistance. Finally, after many years, I was able to help him.

I opened my eyes for the first time since the crash almost two weeks after it happened on March 18, 2012.

My doctor and Joe worked to get me up to speed since I had had breakfast with Dad at the Bagel Hut. It was disturbing that I couldn't respond. Three mini strokes occurred while I was comatose. They impacted my left vocal cord, which caused me to lose my ability to speak. At some point in the near future I made the connection that if I couldn't speak, I certainly couldn't sing anymore, but March 18th wasn't that day. I had so much to tell Joe and the fact that I couldn't was the most upsetting part. My lack of energy and ability to focus upset me, too. It drained me.

After a series of speech lessons with a pathologist, which gave me the ability to speak again, I was able to tell Joe about my journey with Dustin. Our son was in heaven now; he was home. It brought me great joy to share the news with my love. I could see in his eyes that he could perceive my newfound enthusiasm to live and heal from the tragedies.

Did the accident happen so that we could spend one more day together? Was that God's plan? I was open to believing just about anything.

Experiencing the miracle motivated me to go through rehab. After everything we'd already gone through, rehab was going to be a piece of cake.

six

J o e

I'D NEVER HEARD ANYONE SCREAM like that, and I had just spent the better part of three months in the brain rehabilitation ward of a hospital, where a lot of injured people were doing a lot of outrageous things.

It was the Fourth of July. We were at the hospital. It doesn't sound like the ideal place to spend a holiday, but deep down, I was celebrating. Dr. Ahmed had an intern with him who was in training. MaryAnn had finally passed the swallow test, and the G-tube (a feeding tube in her stomach) was being removed. It was a happy day.

Dysphagia, difficulty swallowing, is a common side effect of being intubated for weeks. The doctors had inserted a breathing tube down MaryAnn's trachea for mechanical ventilation in order to keep her alive. She had been intubated and extubated during her first five weeks in the Special Intensive Care Unit, which damaged her vocal cords.

She also suffered three mini strokes, one of which had paralyzed her left vocal cord. As I sat beside her, I often thought about how I couldn't imagine lying in bed with a tube down my throat. I probably would have ripped it out, which is why, I theorized, her hands had been restrained day and night for the entire three weeks after she woke up.

I was overjoyed the day she was able to breath on her own. They extubated her just before Easter Sunday, 2012. The problem was, however, that they had intubated with her left vocal cord in the open position. When they removed the tube permanently, her vocal cord remained somewhat open, as if it had been conditioned to be like that. This meant that all food and fluids would go down the wrong way and enter into her lungs instead of her stomach. Her left vocal cord was serving as a railroad switch. Imagine a train traveling the railway. The vocal cords are like point blades. Now the left one has shifted positions, and so the "train," the food, is directed down the divergent path—to the lungs. In the proper position, food travels through the esophagus and into the stomach. In this new position, the open position, it meant that MaryAnn had to learn how to swallow all over again. Her brain, with the help of the speech pathologist, had to work to retrain the left vocal cord and put it back into the proper resting position. Until she could pass a videoflouroscopy—a swallow study in which doctors would monitor the path of a thickened fluid as it traveled down her throat—she was stuck eating in a nontraditional way. Well, she failed the first videoflouroscopy and had to have a gastrostomy tube (also know as a G-tube) inserted through her belly into her stomach.

She ended up failing the swallow test numerous times, with a three-week spread between tests. This continued through May and June. MaryAnn had to be able to swallow without the risk of choking or coughing, thereby reducing the chance of aspirating into the lungs and developing pneumonia.

She couldn't speak effectively through most of this so I purchased a magnetic alphabet board. With that board, she'd spell out words the best she could. I understood every look, frown, and wave of her finger (more on "that finger" in a little while), but this was exceptionally beneficial for the doctors, nurses, and the rehab team.

My wife was literally starving for months living off a liquid diet inserted right into the stomach. She could smell food—even hospital food smelled like a feast. She experienced hunger around the clock. I felt so bad, but what could I do? The feeding tube is intended to keep people alive, not satiate them.

Finally that day was about to come when MaryAnn could enjoy a cup of coffee in the morning, like the rest of the world. I had been longing for this day like I used to long for candy apples at the carnival when I was a kid, or for Dan Marino to win the Super Bowl. My life had become about moments that actually mattered. This was one of them.

Back in April and May, she would call from the brain trauma unit daily and say, "Where the hell are you?" She'd grunt out the basic sounds of each word. It would be noon. I was at work. I'd come every day after three. That's when I was free, and besides the hospital didn't want me interfering with her rehabilitation, which started at six in the morning and went until three daily. She swore at them incessantly using that little finger of hers. And when she wasn't swearing at them, she was phoning me.

I finally took her phone away and shoved it in the closet on the top shelf in her room when she wasn't looking. One night at about 2:00 a.m., she called to say she missed me very much and needed me by her side. How could I say no? I showed up at six, just before rehab. I wondered how she got the phone all the way to the hospital. That little sneak. Turns out she bribed the nighttime cleaning lady, who rallied a phone so she could wake up her exhausted husband. There's nothing wrong with her brain, I thought.

When I got there, I was greeted with the typical, "Where the hell were you?" salutation. MaryAnn wasn't a naturally pissed off person; she was just starving. She'd ask anybody for anything. The runny hospital pudding looked like crème brûlée to her.

One fine May day, I bucked the system, dodged a few nurses, and got her outside. It didn't stop her from dreaming of steak dinners and apple pie à la mode, but I got a thumbs up and a photo to commemorate the moment.

The only time she wasn't raging mad, hungry to the nth degree, was when another patient would go on a rant. We were in the brain trauma unit. MaryAnn had initial cognitive  impairment. She knew her name and who the president was, but thought her birthday was December 21 (when it was really January 25). A few wrong answers and the traumatic brain injuries she suffered in the accident landed her in that unit.

Thankfully, she was being rehabilitated from home by the time June came. I was sensitive to her nose and stomach and kept the cooking to a minimum. And I enjoyed helping MaryAnn with just about everything. I had never assisted someone physically like this before. No one wants this to happen, trust me, but I discovered I wasn't half bad at giving care to someone I loved, and there was joy in watching her reach milestones, knowing that I helped.

One day, I was pouring in her favorite lunch, a can of Ensure, when she coughed unexpectedly. The entire contents of her stomach shot out of her G-tube and hit me in my face. It smelled awful but it made her laugh. This is not one of the moments of joy to which I was referring, but a funny story in retrospect.

Making her smile felt nice. I was filled with love and hope watching her doze off, finally resting after a long day with a therapist. She wanted to get better. Before the accident the will to live had vacated her soul. I was scared every day. It was back now. She said it was because she got closure, helping Dustin find peace in the Afterlife. Silver linings, I guess.

Like I mentioned, she was finally getting her G-tube removed after four months. Inserting it was a thirty-minute procedure that was performed back in April. A small incision was made in the abdomen and a tube was slid through that hole and into the stomach. Taking that tube out involved a whole different strategy.

I watched as the intern lifted the corner of MaryAnn's blouse and started yanking. She let out a whale of a cry. I nearly lunged at the kid. I gave the doctor a look that required no words. He moved the intern aside and stepped in. Then, before I could flinch an inch closer, he gripped the tube and yanked more violently than the kid had. She let out another cry, a horror movie scream. To make matters worse, the incision had been healing around the G-tube for four months, making it smaller. Once removed, we were able to see what kept the tube in place so well. There was another device, an inch and a half in length, lodged into the feeding tube perpendicularly. This sat like a stopper against the interior wall of her abdomen until it was yanked out.

But MaryAnn could talk now. She could walk again. And now she was going to be able to enjoy the simple pleasure of eating a meal. I couldn't wait to shoot the breeze over a few crackers, some cheese, and a glass of wine. I hope that doesn't sound selfish. I had missed that.

I reflected on the things we take for granted.

Every spring I've wracked my brain to come up with two anniversary presents. I've been doing that for twenty-one years. We got married on May 7, 1994, as planned, but it wasn't official. On Friday May 6, 1994, during the church rehearsal at St. Bartholomew's Cathedral in New York  City, the priest informed me that he couldn't marry us. We had gotten our license in New Jersey but were supposed to have obtained one at NYC Town Hall. The priest advised us to call the wedding off since it wouldn't be legal. It all came down to logistical crap. We had twenty-two friends in our bridal party, all waiting in the back of the church with no idea about what was going on. Plus, we had three hundred guests showing up for the wedding and reception the next day; they were scheduled to come in shifts. The Hilton's rooftop reception hall couldn't accommodate over 200 people. So we literally had to split the group in half—family members from 4:00 to 7:00, friends from 8:00 to midnight. That's how much planning went into the big day. *This wedding was happening.* I emptied my pockets, then gave my best man, Ray Tomasso, the eye, and he emptied his. We made an on-the-spot "donation" to the cause, and with that the priest turned, waved his hand to everyone at the back of the church, and said, "Come on up."

We were married as scheduled the following afternoon. The priest informed us later that we would have to come back after our honeymoon, obtain a NY State license, then go back to the church to get re-married. On June 8, 1994 we were re-married on the books privately in his chambers.

Back at the Hilton, I had reserved the penthouse. After dress rehearsal, management called to inform us that Hillary Clinton sprang into town and that the penthouse was where she normally stayed. My only job was to make this wedding perfect for my bride, so I politely declined their invitation to move. Hillary ended up staying at the Sheraton Hotel next door.

MaryAnn's band was hired for the reception. This was wonderful for two reasons. MaryAnn was able to join them periodically on stage and do what she loved—sing her heart out. That was the first reason. The second reason was that she wasn't singing to anyone but me. That was the best wedding present a guy could've ever asked for.

I want to say it was smooth sailing after that, but it's hard to get New Yorkers, family or not, to leave a party at 7:00 p.m. when the fun's just beginning. Over capacity didn't begin to describe it. By Sunday, we were slapped with massive corking fees from excess champagne. We got another fine because MaryAnn's band was non-union. We had food delivered from outside the hotel after midnight, which was also against policy. Long story short, I got banned from the New York Hilton indefinitely. This wasn't in theory. I went to a Microsoft conference to hear Bill Gates speak a few years later, and a couple big guys in dark suits were waiting for me at the top of the escalator. They must have had facial recognition software in their security system.

Even though MaryAnn didn't remind me repeatedly about the double anniversary dates like she normally did, that memory kept me going on the tougher days. The fear of forgetting one of the two dates (the greatest fear some married men have every year), wasn't weighing on me. My wife was in rehab, recovering from life-threatening injuries due to a senseless car accident. I missed not feeling the pressure of finding primo gifts for our eighteenth anniversar(ies). The theme for seventeen years is furniture. I couldn't tell you what I was supposed to buy in 2012. I got MaryAnn flowers, told her how much I loved her, but it was mostly about wishes. I wished she could walk without assistance. I prayed she got all her memory back. I really prayed that damned feeding tube got removed soon because the day-to-day was hurting my heart. And I wished my wife would be able to sing again soon. This wish was for her. Yes, her voice was magic. It sent me to another place. It made me believe in God and love. I felt luckier than most guys when she sang. I had her heart, and there it was performing for all to see when she sang to nobody but me. But I could live without MaryAnn ever uttering another note in tune. I just wasn't sure she could. Now that

Dustin was gone, I prayed daily that her voice wouldn't be taken away, too. She was born with it, like the rest of us are born with arms and legs. Part of her heart was mutilated in Dustin's suicide. I prayed the other integral parts of her would remain intact. It was a constant wish.

It was summertime, sunny and 80°, an awesome New York day.

The last contraption depriving my wife of her strength and independence had finally been removed. The pain of the evident had dissipated. MaryAnn was no longer screaming. Her breathing was back to normal. A smile was even forming. She was okay again. Her mind, body, and soul were fighting for freedom and winning.

This was the proudest I have ever been of anyone.

It was time to celebrate so I took my wife out for ice cream and a movie.

PART II:

Rain

seven

MaryAnn

AFTER YEARS OF STUDY AND experimentation with my world-renowned vocal coach, Don Lawrence, I was back to learning the basics. I thought that I would never be able to sing again. We had to start from square one. Learning to breathe diaphragmatically, which, by the way, is the natural way we breathe at birth. And, once again, I was learning to place my voice properly. This was not as easy as it sounds because of the paralyzed vocal cord. There was a natural tendency to sing breathy, due to the paralyzation. We worked in a very limited range, not to put any pressure at all on my vocal cords, focusing on the few exercises designed for a person in my situation. After a few short months of this "easy" approach my paralyzed vocal cord started to vibrate on its own. It seemed like a miracle!

Singing is two-part process: mental and physical. Most of us have the capacity to hear simple melodic lines in our musical minds and produce sounds with our God-given instruments, but in order to speak or sing with confidence, good control, power, range, and flexibility, it takes practice.

The new MaryAnn, the survivor, was just happy to be alive. That she could do it wrong seemed like enough for her—just to be able to create sound again. But Don Lawrence did not let the new MaryAnn get in my way. He was hard on me. He wouldn't let me get away with anything. "MaryAnn, that tone is dark," he'd say. "Regardless of how high or low you sing you never place the voice below the palate level." I was getting comfortable, too comfortable. I was starting to not concentrate on what I was doing. I was just singing. I knew that "Practice makes permanent." That was a constant reminder: when I was practicing, every note counted!

And on and on he went, as if he never got the memo, the one about the death of my son, the car accident, the coma, etc. That had to be my favorite thing about him, one of New York City's finest teachers. He didn't treat me any differently than before. I had barely escaped death and my body had had to recover from the ground up, I had started anew just a year back, and although sensitive to my situation, he had a job to do. And what a job he did.

Before the car accident, it was Dustin's death that caused such a stir in people's faces and in their mannerisms upon seeing me. Everyone seemed so uncomfortable and heartbroken. Even my closest friends were so sad; there was no erasing the pain on their faces. Then that grief was compounded by pity after the car accident— I saw heartbreak and pity on every face I encountered after awakening from the coma. They tried to hide it, but it made no difference. And I couldn't even talk, couldn't even say, "Cut the crap, lose the frown, I'm still MaryAnn. You can joke with me, you know, like before." I imagine my face would have contorted like that, too, had one of my dear friends lost a child and then came close to losing her life. I'd be in shock and feel helpless, and maybe in constant debate with the Lord. "Why? Why? Why did so much tragedy happen to this person I care for? She doesn't deserve all this…" Maybe my face would look like it was working overtime to smile, too.

But with my vocal coach? He didn't have any pity. He was business as usual. He took his job seriously. I could've been sitting there in a full body cast and he'd still be barking orders. It felt so good. Going to speech therapy (that's what I called it) was always the highlight of my days, with Joe as my comfort at night.

———————⌒∽⌒———————

I had tried going back to work in September of 2012 after having passed the rehab exams—swallowing, talking, walking. I graduated with my "degree" in walking after successfully climbing up two stairs and back down without any assistance. But back at work, there wasn't a smidgen of sympathy for my situation. Believe it or not, when I was in recovery the whole world of advertising took the final plunge from paper to paperless, from yellow-page advertising to Internet. I had had most clients for twenty years or more. I could have talked them into buying ad space in a satellite that was going to be orbiting the moon and they would have done it. But coworkers had taken over while I was gone. Because of this, most of my accounts had simply vanished or worse, were in the negative. My fellow employees weren't invested in maintaining them. I guess I understood it. This was a commission-based job. Nothing was certain. Their only motivation for covering my accounts while I was gone would have been the satisfaction of helping someone in need, which they were clearly not interested in.

I remember whining about chores in the summertime when I was a kid. "But Mom, it's called summer vacation for a reason! If I vacuum the whole house, can I have a quarter for a freezee at the corner store? I can bike there; you won't have to drive me." Then Mom would say, "No, MaryAnn, you don't get a quarter for helping the family. We all pitch in. We help out. It's what we do. You'll get a whole hot fudge sundae from God when you get to heaven. That'll be your reward for helping out your parents. Not some flimsy popsicle—a whole sundae, with pecans and everything. Now get to work!"

Upon my return, I was responsible for turning these cancelled contracts around, but between the grief I was actively feeling over Dustin again and my inability to multi-task like I used to, my brain was not prepared for this added pressure. By February of 2013 another cognitive evaluation rendered me impaired and I was put on disability.

That was over six months ago. It's been wonderful not having to go to that job any longer.

Making my own way in the world was always something that was ingrained in me by my parents, and thank God, it's kept my pride intact while I've played the waiting game with my music career. I've contributed. But the release my body has experienced from not having to go to a place that has never made me feel at home has been the biggest therapy of all.

The downside to that kind of stress vacating the terrain of my mind was that it left so much open space, and more memories of Dustin occupied it in no time.

I wouldn't have called it obsessed, but I had nothing to gauge it by. I held on tight to the dream I had had of my son, walking hand in hand to heaven, but time was making those images grainy and fading them faster than constant exposure to the desert sun could have. So I turned my focus to tangible memories: Dustin's professional photos. He had taken pictures of everything—people, buildings, birds, a perfect drop of rain on the New York sidewalk. My son captured images of the whole wide world before he died, and they should all be on display. They all tell a special story.

Joe said I was turning the whole place into a shrine.

Our Father, who art in heaven,
Hallowed be thy name.
Thy kingdom come,
Thy will be done, on earth as it is in heaven.

That was my new life: work-free days sometimes sprinkled with Speech Therapy, missing Dustin, anticipating Joe's return home just before sunset, and then reciting the Perfect Prayer before closing my eyes every night.

I was grateful to be alive. And on the gloomier days, when I missed my son too much, I reminded myself how much Dad and Joe loved me. And that brought me peace.

eight

Joe

IT FELT LIKE GOING BACK to work took a bite out of Mar-yAnn's soul. Her emotional state seemed to dip back to where it was a year and a half ago when she was at her worst, between Dustin's death and the accident. It wasn't good. Not having to go to her nine to five anymore was better, and having a voice trainer was the best. But all the *do re mi's* in the world couldn't fill the cracks in her delicate heart.

Tomorrow will be better; that's what you have to keep telling yourself. It was the fall of 2013, and the holidays are never good on anyone suffering from great loss like we were, but we did what we did best and planned an epic feast anyway. *Back to normal. This could be great.* Historically, we've hosted Thanksgiving and Christmas Eve. Family and friends are precious, and having them around would keep our minds off the events that had consumed the last nineteen months of our lives. Our circle of friends, or at least most of them, has stuck by us through everything. There are some that fell by the wayside, not knowing what to say. We didn't have another child. You wouldn't believe how common conversations are about one's children are until your only son is gone. For some people it was easier not to invite us to the party. They worried about accidentally asking how Dustin was; telling us about their son's engagement or daughter's recent law degree was just too much. Mostly, that wasn't the case.

One night when MaryAnn and I were enjoying a glass of wine and updating one of the Bungalow Foundation's web pages, she said, "We sure do have wonderful friends, Joe. They've given us so much love and support."

"I agree. We're really lucky, Mare. If we had a stack of hundred dollar bills and handed them out to all our friends for safekeeping, how many do you think would be able to return that same bill, same serial number, ten years later?"

MaryAnn and I starting counting on our fingers. We lost track after ten.…. That was the moment it occurred to us to get back into the mix a bit more. We wanted to show our thanks, get back to normal, and make a conscious effort to let our friends and family know they were loved and appreciated. A Thanksgiving feast? Okay, why not? Life was calming down, and once again, we were planning a holiday dinner.

Between work, helping MaryAnn, and making holiday plans, I'd give thanks to the Lord that my wife was recovering, and then remind myself of the law of threes to calm down my insides. Everybody's heard that bad things happen in threes. After the crash of 2008, when we almost lost everything, we had just recovered when Dustin died. Back then it didn't hit me to "stay tuned" for one more disaster…because things happen in threes. I didn't think like that back then. But MaryAnn and Artie's accident sure made that myth a reality. Now that we were three-time tragedy survivors, I was ready to celebrate, just a little. It seemed like the coast was clear.

On November 8, 2013, Mare had a vision seizure at 8:30 in the morning. It lasted about an hour. I told her we should head over to the hospital for an MRI just to be on the safe side. After all, she had suffered a horrific auto accident with severe head trauma not too long ago. But MaryAnn didn't want to go for fear that they'd keep her over the weekend, as most hospitals do when you check in on a Friday and they find something. So I called MaryAnn's neurologist. He recommended we contact her primary care doctor and get a script for an MRI ASAP. So that afternoon we went to her primary care doctor and asked for a script for an MRI of the brain. Since MaryAnn also had vision issues, we went to see her optometrist, Dr. Buchman. He noted the left field of vision had been reduced since Mare's last visit and suggested there might be a brain issue. He also thought an MRI was in order. That was already booked for the following day. I didn't realize it then, but it's important to get an eye exam every year because it can reveal so much, including diabetes, hypertension, autoimmune disorders, high cholesterol, thyroid disease, cancer, and tumors.

On November 14, after the MRI, it was discovered that MaryAnn had a massive glioblastoma multiforme, 3 x 3.5 x 4 centimeters, in her right posterior temporal craniotomy.

"Are you kidding me?" I asked myself. Not again! This poor girl. I felt so helpless. I love her so much. The thought of her having to go through more physical and emotional pain was more than I could bear. *It's not fair! When was this going to end? What do I do now? What doctor do we go to? What hospital do we go to? Who's the best brain surgeon? What the hell is a glioblastoma multiforme?*

I wasn't going to let anything happen to her. That was the only truth left inside me. There was no way we weren't going to beat this thing, whatever it was. On the inside, a small voice ehoed, telling me it was a death sentence. But on the outside, I reiterated, "Everything is going to be fine. We've gone through fire in the past, and this is just a little rain, Mare. Just a little rain...."

We didn't rush into anything. We took a few days to investigate options. We had Duke running clinical trials on one thing, MD Anderson running trials on another, MGH on immunotherapy, Fox Chase working on custom therapy cocktails, RWJ looming with a gamma knife, Dr. Leferman with radio surgery, and Sloan Kettering with all of the above. Where to go? What to do? Who to choose? We listened to them all, and then Al Messano, a trusted friend, introduced us to one of the very best brain surgeons, who happened to be at Sloan Kettering right here in New York. So there we went. It was confirmed through the eyes of a surgeon who had performed over 10,000 brain surgeries that it was a glioblastoma multiforme.

f Joe Anselmo

November 16, 2013

There's no easy way to say this, and believe me I love answering your phone calls, but right now we need to concentrate on the most important matter at hand, which is MaryAnn. For those of you who do not know, MaryAnn's latest MRIs reveal a rather large glioblastoma in her brain. It needs immediate surgery. Her stress level needs to be kept at a minimum to relax her brain in order for the procedure to go as smoothly as possible. If you do feel the need to tak with her, please remember: be positive!! Don't keep her on the phone too long, and keep the content cheerful. With God's blessings and your prayers, pathology will tell us it's only a benign meningioma, and no further post-surgery treatment will be required.

On November 25, 2013, we arrived at Sloan Kettering for MRIs, a chest X-ray, and pre-registration. The following day, Mare was admitted at 10:30 a.m. for surgery. My brothers and sisters stayed with us while we waited. Surgery was scheduled for 1:00 p.m. that day.

The minutes passed like days. We had a private waiting room that easily sat fifteen to twenty people, but it felt like we were stuffed into a closet. I can't describe it any better than that. My stomach ached like when I was young—filled with that sick sensation of having just been broken up with. My heart lay wounded in the pit of my stomach. Helpless. My mind was flooded with thoughts of MaryAnn, good times and bad, but mostly good. God, how I love her.

At 9:00 p.m., my family and I are gathered in one of the post-op waiting rooms when MaryAnn's surgeon and his assistant finally entered. He told me he successfully resected 75% of the tumor, but had to leave the rest for fear of affecting her motor skills, vision, and speech. Then he briefed me and set my expectations of how long she would be in recovery, how long before she could leave the hospital, follow up appointments, her diet, and how I should care for her wound and dressings. They started for the door and I realized that he never spoke about her prognosis. They never speak about the prognosis. And you know what? Most people don't ask. They don't want to know. Why would they want to disrupt their perfect picture of their life?

"Hold on, Doc, what about her prognosis?" I asked.

He turned and came back into the room. "By the looks of her tumor it's a high-grade glioblastoma multiforme and she has one year, maybe two at most."

It felt like someone had hit me with a sledgehammer. Two years? No way, not MaryAnn. This wasn't going to happen to her. Everything was going to be fine. Now I know why no one asks.

It was late and my family had to head back to Jersey. Twelve hours of waiting and pacing around that claustrophobic waiting room was exhausting. They didn't want to leave but I told them I would be fine. I wasn't fine, though. I was mush. I wanted to crawl under a piece of furniture, go to sleep, and wake up in the morning to all of this being a bad dream. The worst dream ever. I could not wish this on my worst enemy.

I was alone in the room as I waited for MaryAnn to wake up from surgery, which no longer felt like a closet. The seats had multiplied and the walls had stretched out and away like a balloon. The space was endless. Silence and solitude do strange things.

Finally, at 10:30, a nurse brought me to see MaryAnn in a post-op intensive care unit.

MaryAnn was answering questions from the nursing staff to check her level of alertness. She knew today's date and who the president was. All vitals were good. But when the staff asked if she knew where she was, she said she was in the basement of her childhood home in Oakland, New Jersey with our son Dustin and her mom, Terry. She said they were sitting on the corner of the bed watching over her. Spooky. It made me think about the Afterlife.

Mare's spirits were low the next morning. She was in a little pain and didn't want to leave her bed but she had no choice because OT and PT therapists had her up and around. She didn't want to sit in a chair and later refused OT testing. MRIs were scheduled and she couldn't miss those. I arrived at 8:00 a.m. and stayed until midnight.

Mare's spirits were a little better by Thursday but she still didn't want to leave her bed. I bribed her with foot massages, but only if she sat in the chair, which she did.

So there we were, celebrating Thanksgiving in the hospital, just the two of us. The food was wonderful, which was a nice treat. Just as desert was being served we heard a familiar voice coming down the hallway. Frank Clark, his wife, Julie, and their two kids, Erica and Heidi, had flown in from Kentucky. Wow, what a surprise! On Thanksgiving. How incredible and selfless. We are so blessed to have good friends.

Besides prayer, Frank Clark was my saving grace. If I used up 1,000 minutes a week on my phone during Maryann's six-week stay in SICU after her accident, 90% of them were to my buddy, Frank. He translated all her doctors' medical terminology into lyrics I could understand. We had met on the beaches of Cancun about thirty-five years ago. I was in the water when something hit me. I'll never forget it. It fell from the sky, torpedoing right at me. As fate would have it, that incident connected Frank and me forever. It was a Frisbee. And when I returned it to its rightful owners, Frank and his cousin, they asked me to join in the game.

I was staying at a co-op that belongs to my friend Ken in NYC during Mare's three-night hospital stay. On pickup day, I arrived at Sloan at 8:00 a.m. with Mare's outdoor wear (scarf, coat, hat, and gloves). We were given home instructions and checked out at 2:30 p.m. Unbelievable! Brain surgery on Tuesday and out by Friday. Unfortunately, that day pathology confirmed a high-grade glioblastoma multiforme. The tumor was malignant.

I quickly began making calls to determine the best cutting edge treatments available for glioblastomas. These were some of my early discoveries:

1. Vaccine treatments could be done with DNA sequencing, which is tumor-specific genetic alterations that can potentially be matched to precision drugs. That was happening at Fox Chase in Philly and Sloan Kettering in NY.

2. Stem cell treatment

3. Other treatments utilizing the body's natural defense systems, such as Dr Bruzyinski's treatment

But on Christmas day, MaryAnn started chemo as planned. I was spending most of my time educating myself on all alternative therapies. I hate chemo and what it does to the entire immune system but we had to stick with the traditional treatment plan initially. For us, any treatment was better than none because it felt like forward motion, whether or not it actually was. Knowing what I know now, I wouldn't have rushed into radiation and chemo. Some practitioners know this, some don't, yet it mostly comes down to making money. The system is damaged.

The following day, December 26, six weeks of radiation began.

Within a few days, MaryAnn was so sick that she couldn't get out of bed. I had to take leave from work again. She was responding adversely to the Temozolomide (chemotherapy). It was clear that this form of treatment was going to kill my wife long before the tumor did. She was terminal, but the doctors said chemo and radiation would extend the fatal diagnosis some. The prognosis was twelve to twenty-four months. Surgery, radiation, and ongoing chemotherapy for twelve to twenty-four months? That was going to be the rest of MaryAnn's life? Bedridden, unable to eat, sick, and vomiting? Too weak to enjoy even the simplest of pleasures in life? A cup of coffee, reading a book by the bay window, holding my hand while watching a movie—those things were gone? That life is not for my wife!

Worse than that, it didn't seem like MaryAnn was going to make it to New Year's if chemo continued. I couldn't take it. I couldn't watch her die. By the second week of January 2014, her platelets had dropped below 50 and she was taken off the chemotherapy. Her body rejected it; the radiation continued but the chemo stopped. *Now what?* It seemed every doctor at all the best hospitals had the same recipe for brain cancer—surgery, followed by radiation and chemo.

There had to be another way.

Things were supposed to happen in threes. I couldn't believe this. Did the economic bubble in 2008 not count as one of our three tragedies? Was it because it was financial, and not a health crisis? Is the pattern of threes deeper and more specific than we think? Or, are MaryAnn and I less lucky than the average person, and so a fourth tragedy occurred? Are we the exception to this rule—the one that's been around for thousands of years? Maybe it's as simple as that: things happen in threes except for a few really unlucky bastards. For them, the hits just keep on coming.

One night when I was trying to make sense of it all, it occurred to me that maybe everything else—the economic crash, Dustin's death, the car accident—was preparing me for this, the catastrophe of all catastrophes. God knows I'm a different man now than I was two years ago.

There I was again, by my bride's bedside, watching her suffer with an incurable brain tumor. I was still a numbers guy, though, and this didn't add up. I was sad, angry, and questioning God's motives. We had had our hardships. The bad times were supposed to be over, at least for a little while longer. I was steaming mad. And most of all, I wished it were me. She had been through enough. My Mare had been through enough. If this had to happen, why couldn't it have happened to me? I ask God to pick me to be the victim this time.

nine

MaryAnn

I HAD A VIVID DREAM about Dustin's new whereabouts. The act of his suicide two years ago, back in 2012, has never stopped weighing heavy on my heart. Maybe it sounds silly to even state that. Naturally, it weighed on me. I had other things going on, however, like brain cancer. Still, memories of my son took precedence, and that was okay. The part of my brain that wasn't being taken over by pesky, misbehaving mutating cells was consumed by thoughts of Dustin.

The dream was brilliant and detailed like our walk to Heaven. In the dream, I could see myself as if I was outside my body watching a scene on a stage in a grand amphitheater. I was opening up a set of double doors to his old wardrobe closet, the one that he had hung himself in. But to my surprise, as I swung those doors wide, a stunning body of water in the shade of admiral blue, deep, rich, clean, lay before me.

I dove in! Even though the water looked icy and fresh, it was warm. As I started to swim, the beach came into focus with its rich, opalescent sands. That must be Paradise. My son is there! He finally fulfilled his dream of surfing the waters of Habushi-ura! I felt the Lord's presence and thanked him for making my son's dream come true. The realization that Dustin's Heaven was a beach in Japan was as clear as the silky waters massaging my limbs.

I cranked my neck around to get a full-circle view of my son's new home. Opposite the beach was a glacier with a flock of penguins marching about. Even in my dream, I could hear the voice in my head: *What's up with that?* And then that other voice answered: *Well, you know, penguins do mate for life.* Could these loyal, regal, devoted penguins be watching over my Dustin in the Afterlife? Works for me. Satisfied and reassured of Dustin's well-being, I turned around and swam back toward the double doors.

I knew everything was going to be fine with my brain. Maybe I was too sick to worry, too tired to care. Maybe I was in too much pain to think about the future. Through MRIs, surgery, test results, chemo, and radiation, no one mentioned anything about me "getting my ducks in a row," or "my papers in order." No one used the word "terminal." Maybe that's why I had a sense of calm. I would later discover, much later in this journey, that Joe prohibited that kind of talk around me. Maybe that's what did it—Joe's love was so strong it overpowered my fear.

I don't have all the answers. If I did, I'd understand more about the last decision Dustin ever made. I just knew that I was going to have a story to share, even at this early stage, even so sick from chemo that I couldn't sit up. It hurt to be awake. As I dozed off again, I caught myself adding Niijima Island to the bucket list in my head. That's how strong my resolution was to beat this thing.

ten

Joe

LESS THAN 1% OF THE population will ever be diagnosed with a brain tumor. Yet that minuscule percentage still means that almost 700,000 Americans are living with one today. Seventy thousand people get diagnosed annually, with twenty thousand of those tumors turning up malignant. There's less than a 25% chance of surviving brain cancer beyond the first year. It's not good. Standard treatment is surgical resection, radiation, and chemotherapy using Temozolomide. If a person is over seventy, surgery is often bypassed, and they start chemo and radiation instead. What about the other 50,000 people diagnosed with a benign brain tumor? If the tumor is growing, it, too, has to be surgically removed in most cases. Chemo may not be necessary, but if the tumor continues to grow they will need to address that issue. What then? Radiation? And what if the tumor is inoperable and surgery is out of the question? What then? Radiation still kills brain cells—the good and the bad ones.

I have a friend, Mark, who has a benign brain tumor. He started having vision problems and they discovered a tumor pressing up against his optic nerve. Doctors recommended surgical resection, but that was a dangerously impossible option. He went through with the surgery anyway and it was successful. This improved his quality of life for two solid years. Then he started losing his eyesight again, which meant that the tumor had started growing again. This new tumor growth was diagnosed as completely inoperable. I asked if his doctors ran genetic tests. He said they did not. He had signed forms donating his tissue to research with no direct benefit to him. This is what most people do. I told Mark to contact pathology and see if they still had his tissue in cold storage. If so, demand the intention of the donation be changed from "research" to "clinical biopsy" in order to learn the specifics about the tumor. A few days later, he confirmed the tissue sample was in their possession (not yet sent to research). He requested a change in his donation intention. Luckily, Mark can now have his doctor order full genetic sequencing. This is personalized medicine. My friend has a chance. Maybe they'll find what can stop his tumor growth, save his sight, and improve the length and quality of his life. His tumor will be treated, like MaryAnn's was, based on its own composition. It's not simply lumped into the category of brain tumor and treated using textbook protocol. This is our future.

However, most doctors will still recommend radiation. Well, I'm here to tell you that radiation is no joke. It's going to kill good brain cells. My only advice is that you should research all options thoroughly. It's not an emergency in that you have two hours to figure out a new life plan. Don't rush into surgery or radiation right away. Take a week or two and do serious research.

Every doctor in every hospital said the same thing to MaryAnn: surgery, radiation, chemo. Why is that? Did they all go to the same school? Or is it because of the socialization of medicine, lousy insurance coverage, and doctors making less money? Is it hospital policy/procedure to perform surgery, radiation, chemo? Is it protocol for everyone in all oncology departments to recommend this? Is it standard?

I'm not categorizing all doctors as defaulting to "standard procedure" in all circumstances. My father was a doctor but his patients were his first priority. He swore by the Hippocratic Oath, one of the oldest documents in history and one that all doctors must swear by. Do all hold it true in their hearts? Do money and mainstream techniques take over after a time? If I only knew then what I know now, we would have never opted for radiation. The research I was able to do on my own led me to ask the questions that led us to the discovery of the genetic mutation that was responsible for MaryAnn's tumor growth. The clinical trial we finally found *specific to that mutation* shrunk her tumor from 1.8 centimeters (after surgery had resected 75% and post radiation) to zero, nada, nothing, gone. No more tumor! Do the research, and perhaps there's another option before radiation, or in addition to radiation, and if that doesn't work then radiation could still be available. I'm not professing to know anything about medicine, and I believe doctors are our saving hope, but in MaryAnn's case she probably did not need radiation. Her body and mind would have been better served had we bypassed it altogether. You need to ask your doctors for all the options beyond standard protocol. And get another opinion, and another opinion, and another opinion. We interviewed four surgeons before making our decision. Then after surgery, I had samples of MaryAnn's brain tissue sent to four different hospitals for genetic sequencing.

After you hear a term like glioblastoma multiforme and you get past the disbelief and shock phase, you go home and Google it. That's when you begin to face statistics that are not pleasant.. It's terrifying. Cancer. Brain cancer. I kept thinking if I was the one with a diagnosis of cancer, I could manage it if the tumor was anywhere but my brain. I could look down at the cancer in my lung, stomach, colon, talk to it, threaten it, let it know its days inside my body are limited, tell it to start packing its bags. But with brain cancer, how can you separate yourself? All I wanted for MaryAnn was rest and a positive attitude. We had had the surgery and she was handling the radiation just fine. That was to be ongoing until the end of February. After that, we had to wait thirty days before starting any new kind of treatment. This gave me almost ten weeks to do more research for a cure or better alternative for my wife.

My biggest ally besides my drive and devotion to MaryAnn was that Sloan Kettering Cancer Center had the tumor tissue safely in storage.

You sign your life away when someone you love goes into brain surgery. I cannot tell you how many of my John Hancocks branded the documents necessary to let MaryAnn go under the knife. One of these documents was a waiver releasing her tumor and all of its tissue to research. Most hospitals work in conjunction with a university. This is how breakthroughs happen, vaccines are created, and cures are discovered. It's a standard waiver. Everyone going into surgery to resect a tumor or any foreign body signs this form. I signed it. Then a few days later, by the Grace of God, a friend informed me that we should not let MaryAnn's tumor tissue be donated to science without the benefit of knowing the results. We should turn back time and make sure it stays in our care. It hadn't been a week since her surgery. Someone told me we had seven days to change our minds about donating the tumor to science. I don't know how true that is but nevertheless I called the hospital, went down, and reversed our decision. It was now Sloan Kettering's responsibility to keep the tumor tissue safe in storage for us. They were allowed to send it to research but the results were to be shared with us.

The irony of hindsight being 20/20 hit me fast and hard in the weeks following MaryAnn's surgery. It didn't take much investigative work before I regretted allowing my wife to go under the knife in the first place. I was able to rescind donation of the tumor to research, but I couldn't take that move back—going into surgery. I did my best to put a positive spin on that decision: she would have needed some kind of "invasion" in order to get a tumor sample, so I let that go. I had to let everything go that wasn't positive or didn't serve my cause, which was saving MaryAnn's life.

After gaining a working knowledge of what exactly a high grade glioblastoma multiforme was, I started investigating all possible alternate treatments for a brain tumor that was grade three or worse.

There was no medical center in the world that cost too much or was too far away for me to consider. I even contacted a scientist in Jerusalem. He had developed a way to separate THC from CBD in marijuana. Cannabis oil can then be used in high concentrations without the worry of the high in treating various diseases. CBD is such a magnificent anti-inflammatory that it's been known to stop tumor growth and even cure people of numerous aliments. He suggested I find an alternative therapy then try radiation and chemotherapy if need be. We discussed the many different treatments that were in clinical trials in Israel and Spain. I researched the use of CBD oil as an anti-inflammatory to be used as a complementary drug. I was increasing my knowledge base where tumors and treatments were concerned daily.

Every new lead drove me to discover something new. Foxx Chase Cancer Center had a custom cocktail they had developed through genetic sequencing. It turned out Sloan Kettering Cancer Center had a trial study, too. This was for people with latent stage glioblastoma multiformes who had a mutation called BRAF. This was a type of melanoma cancer cell. (More on this in a bit.)

We had MaryAnn's tumor. It wasn't donated to science. We started genetic sequencing—an integrated genomic analysis of her glioblastoma multiforme. Genomic sequencing is very specific, elaborate profiling of the tissue's DNA. When detectives profile a person, they find every possible thing about them: what they look like, where they like to hang out, what they read, where they work, what they do for fun, who they're related to, etc. This creates a basic profile. Profiling a tumor determines its DNA sequence, but only generally. With MaryAnn's tumor, scientists created the same kind of profile, but then went deeper with a process called whole genomic sequencing, which identifies the chromosomal DNA and the DNA inside the mitochondria. Profiling a gene results in learning approximately 1% about that gene. Full genomic sequencing teaches scientists 95% or more about that gene. This is the future of personalized medicine. Check out The Bungalow Foundation, a 501(c)(3) dedicated to funding Biomedical Precision Medicine Initiatives (www.TheBungalow.org). This serves as not only a predictor of diseases that could arise in the body, but whole genomic sequencing can also determine how a tumor reacts to any type of therapeutic treatment by understanding its personal sequence, and then experimenting with different drugs and therapies to see how the tumor cells react and respond. It's a hit or miss process. A scientist applying this new method to tumor tissue could try up to 500 different agents developed in treating mutated cells to see which ones have a positive effect (stop or reverse the growth) on the tumor tissue.

MaryAnn's tumor was discovered to have three mutations. A mutation happens when a normal cell misbehaves and starts to grow. One of her mutations was a gene called BRAF. This human gene creates a protein called B-Raf (or protooncogene, or B-Raf murine sarcoma viral oncogene homolo B). This mutated protein sends signals to the cells it invades and tells them to grow. This mutation, the BRAFV600, is the gene responsible for melanoma. Two drugs have been developed by the FDA in treating later stage melanoma: vemurafenib and dabrafenib. Coincedentally, Sloan Kettering Cancer Center's basket trial was using these drugs to fight against the BRAFV600 gene (melanoma cells) specifically. Their basket trial was not limited to a specific cancer but to all cancers with this mutation, including MaryAnn's glioblastoma multiforme. This is where it gets really interesting: There were patients with lung, colon, and other cancers in the study, too. The main qualification for acceptance into the basket trial was that your tumor was, in part, made up of the BRAFV600 mutation.

There were still two other mutations to consider. MaryAnn's genomic sequencing turned up three, as I mentioned. The thing was the BRAF gene was the rarest. It was anybody's guess which mutated cells were the alphas in her brain, dominating the malignant tumor growth.

We had a feeling. That's all we had to go on—a feeling that the BRAF gene was the cause. Also, the other trials I had investigated that were focusing on the two more common mutations weren't as hopeful about the possibility of life extension.

Dr. David Hyman welcomed my girl into the new trial at Sloan Kettering. It was the beginning of April 2014, thirty days after radiation had been completed.

eleven

M a r y A n n

I WAS MESMERIZED BY THE orchestra as it rose before my eyes at Radio City Music Hall. It was my first date with Mom and we were both dressed to the nines. Earlier that morning, I was looking out our kitchen apartment window when I spotted Grandmother Agnes hustling down 96th Street with shopping bags swinging in each arm. Grandma, a gifted seamstress, had constructed dresses for Mom and me on her Singer. Grandma loved fashion. She sprang into our unit and said, "Surprise!" She wanted us to look our best for the big date. And we did in our snazzy holiday outfits.

My mom, in her ivory satin A-line was reminiscent of Natalie Wood—a real stunner. She turned the heads of men and women alike as she glided down the aisle with her "little Shirley Temple" in the new red jumper. Even though I had gone to see the animated film that followed, I was surprised to discover how I reacted to the headliner...and the orchestra. Goose bumps covered me from head-to-toe. I swear I had them on my ears! That's the moment I became hooked on live music. Then when the goosies settled, a sensation started in my stomach, like butterflies do, and traveled like fish in a tank, shooting off in all directions in my body, consuming me with bliss. *That's going to be me on that stage someday.* I wanted to make people forget about their worries, make them shiver with delight, make them believe their dreams can come true, too.

Grandma surprised me with a roll of coins in my jumper pocket. After the show, I nabbed a tuna fish sandwich out of the glass compartment at the Automat. Kids loved the Automat in the fifties and sixties before McDonald's and Burger King came to be. Mom kept saying, "Don't talk with your mouth full, MaryAnn," but I couldn't help it. I had so much to say about my first experience at Radio City Music Hall.

I had that same sensation of goose bumps and butterflies when I was accepted into Dr. Hyman's basket trial at Sloan Kettering Cancer Center. I knew I was working against the odds. I knew that the waters weren't tested by the masses. Hardly anyone else was doing this. I understood the risks and that I was stepping into mostly un-explored territory in the field of cancer treatment. It didn't matter. Euphoria encapsulated my heart when I got the news.

I lay in bed, too sick to sit up from the chemo, but felt the faith nonetheless, except it was magnified by comparison.

One hundred and twenty-two cancer patients with tumors in places like their brains, lungs, colons were accepted into this trial. There were fifteen different types of cancer among us. We had one thing in common: We were in the latent stages of the disease, and we all carried the BRAFV600 mutation.

I was put on vemurafenib (Zelboraf is the brand name). This drug has been successful in helping 50% of patients with late stage melanoma—the deadliest form of skin cancer.

Like all drugs, there are side effects. My body rejected Te-mozolomide so I had some concerns about vemurafenib. There were many of the same side effects, including hair loss, nausea, and fatigue. But my body didn't reject it. In fact, it started working im-mediately. Joe and I noticed improvements in my cognitive func-tion, including my piano skills. My piano skills! And Dr. Hyman started reporting good news from the onset. This new treatment was shrinking my tumor steadily. Within nine months he would in-form us it was down to the size of a pea.

As vemurafenib got busy destroying that tumor, it was becom-ing ever clear that music was not my only destiny. I had worked a lifetime to gain recognition in the field; anyone could tell you that. But that wasn't because I was drawn to the idea of fame. Singing was a form of self-expression and the basis of my identity. Nothing had ever felt more right. I often wondered why the road was so rocky. Why couldn't I just achieve my dream of performing at Carnegie Hall? I had come so close with Chico's House of Jazz before my dear son died. I wondered about that, too.

Time Magazine got wind of the Sloan Kettering basket trial and my participation and progress. While my lifelong journey as a musician hadn't yet gotten me onto the stages I thought it would, attention had found me in a different way. Don't get me wrong; I'm a big believer in the importance of all forms of art. I'm a painter, too. Art is a necessary part of life. It heals. It beautifies our world. I've always loved touching people with my voice, speaking to their hearts, lifting them through music. But battling terminal cancer is a story for everyone. You don't have to be into music to appreciate a cancer survivor's tale. I had dreamed my musical endeavors would have impact and now they do. I had enough notoriety as a jazz singer to stand out in a sea of terminally ill cancer patients. And my Joe had the drive and instinct to navigate this journey by choosing the right treatment option for me, which helped me beat the odds. His love, along with destiny and timing, created this perfect scenario. Not all hospitals have clinical trials. Joe can tell you: hospitals need funding and bodies to fill slots to even launch clinical trials. What were the chances that the doctor who resected my brain tumor was running a basket trial that I was a perfect candidate for? This trial was right in our backyard. Less than 5% of all people diagnosed with a brain tumor have this option—genetic testing available in their area. It's so new. The American Society of Clinical Oncology is preparing for the future. They've started a registry of patients who've been treated by drugs that were not designed for their type of cancer, but designed to treat the mutated gene discovered through whole genomic testing of their tumor's tissue. They are just now starting to keep track of these findings.

This is what I knew while spending the first year on vemurafenib in Dr. David Hyman's basket trial: I was feeling a little bit stronger every day. I was slowly gaining some of my focus back. I was able to get out of bed daily, make a cup of coffee, go for a walk with Joe, and play the piano. I had strength to continue vocal therapy. At night, near the end of the first year, we were able to enjoy a glass of wine together. Just be us. These are my everyday miracles. Thanks to God's plan, the power of precision medicine, faith, and the love of a good man, I'm able to celebrate life.

MARYANN PICKED UP PAINTING AGAIN
POST-SURGERY
January 2014

twelve

Joe

GOD INTERVENES. I HAVE ALWAYS believed that.

Upon diagnosis of MaryAnn's brain tumor, we had already been through so much that I was ready. I guess it could have gone the other way. I could have been exhausted but I wasn't. I was ready. I was back at church regularly. That hadn't happened since I was a kid. My faith was stronger than it had ever been. The wedding vows had really been tested, and I had stepped up. Plus, my nose was in the books, learning everything I could about other medical conditions—body dysmorphic disorder, comas, cognitive impairment—

for two years before having to roll up my sleeves again and study cancer, cancer treatment options, and glioblastomas (specifically), like I was preparing for board certification. I'm lucky I was built with this kind of tenacity. God is great. I'm even more blessed I was given a fighter for a wife. She's my hero.

Things don't happen in threes. But everything does happen for a reason.

I don't know why Dustin passed and went to the Afterlife so young; I haven't worked that out yet. But I understand the path we've been on since his death in a way that would not have been possible had we not held hands, prayed, kept a positive attitude, and depended on love to beat death so that we could be here together, sharing our story.

MaryAnn's father, Artie, moved in with us after Dustin died. We had tried for years to get him closer to "home," especially after his wife passed. He wouldn't budge. He had lived in his home in Oakland for forty years. He built it! There was no way he was moving out without a fight. After Dustin died, Artie didn't have his "roommate" to lend him a hand with household tasks. Plus, he was devastated. So by mid-February of 2012, he moved in with us. Dad insisted on a nice, big walk-in closet for his stuff, of which there was plenty! Don't get me started on that. But we happily added a closet to his area of the house. This is where facts start to really turn into fate.

Artie insisted on paying for the add-on closet out of his own pocket. I knew I'd never hear the end of it if I didn't let him. He also insisted on paying cash. Who pays cash anymore? He was old school. That's how he talked MaryAnn into the Bagel Hut that day—her first venture out since Dustin's death. He needed to go to the bank to get cash to pay the construction guys for the add-on.

The older gentlemen in the '92 Toyota that T-boned MaryAnn and Artie was also rushed to the hospital. He was given a CAT Scan to eliminate the possibility of internal bleeding, which is how his cancer was discovered. That accident saved his life. He was so grateful that he didn't even try to fight the insurance in court. He took full blame. It was this insurance money that allowed us to stay afloat through all the medical bills, drugs, hospitalizations, and rehab.

Let me take you back for a minute: MaryAnn had what was diagnosed as a *brain angioma* in 1995. We knew a lesion was there. I'll never know for sure if it was the trauma of the car accident that launched its aggressive growth, because sometimes I think it could've been the shock of Dustin's death. Just as all things are possible through faith and positive thinking, all things, too, can happen from ongoing grief. In any case, how would we have ever discovered MaryAnn's tumor without the horrific car accident? We may not have caught it in time. A dizzy spell might not have taken us to the hospital were we not already "regulars."

If MaryAnn's body hadn't rejected chemo after surgery, I wouldn't have looked outside her current medical regimen for options. Who knows how long she would have continued treatment....

There are things in life—these are the real obstacles—that take us from our life path. MaryAnn's brain tumor was not one of them. That was part of our fate as a couple—to manage her health crisis with faith, hope, love, and precision medicine. To think outside the box, believe in miracles, trust our instincts, never give up, and show the world that options exist—this is our life path. We are bigger than our mutated cells; knowledge is everywhere. Look beyond your backyard. Don't be afraid to take risks. Listen to God's voice in your heart. Love with all your might. Trust your own path. Everything happens for a reason.

MaryAnn went into remission in March of 2015. Her MRI showed no trace of a tumor but the cancer cells may still exist in her brain. We know that 80% of most cancers return. We also know that eighteen to twenty-four months was the optimum prognosis she was given, which is how long she would have survived if she had done a chemotherapy and radiation regimen. And now my wife is tumor-free.

That is joy.

THE LOFT OF WILLIAM RILEY
NPR NEWS TAPING "LIVING WITH CANCER" SERIES
March 26, 2015

thirteen

MaryAnn

I Believe in Miracles

Dear Dad,

YOUR PRAYERS HAVE BEEN ANSWERED by Our Father who art in Heaven! It's a miracle, Dad. You worshipped Him all your years, as a devout Catholic in the practice of prayer. In return, He has granted your single, greatest wish: He has extended your little girl's life, once again! I am tumor free, Dad. The Spirit of the Lord taught you to ask for my remission in the Perfect Prayer before you died, and because of your deep faith, my faith has been revitalized to trust in God and move forward in a brighter, more significant way. I am now in remission. Joe and I are making it "through the fire," just as my first song predicted. Through the loss of Dustin, the car accident, stage four brain cancer, and the loss of both Mom and you, we've survived the clinical trial and made it through the fire. We have our whole lives in front of us now to appreciate what God planned and to manifest the vision of my life that you have always dreamed for me.

I believe in miracles, Dad, because I was born your daughter. That was my first encounter with the Divine and His powers that sent me into the arms of you and Mom. Then I was given another miracle. Who knew I was so deserving of so much? This one was more unusual. Some people might not have even recognized it but those people weren't raised by a man like you; their eyes weren't trained to see this sort of thing. I was granted the miracle of sharing my life on earth with a loving husband named Joe. He was "the man in my future," the one you had always dreamed of, the right kind of husband, as you had often referred.

Joe: a fellow of indescribable charm, who has made it a priority to take care of his darling wife before himself.

Does that remind you of anyone you know? He would have made Mom proud. Who knew the evening I made Joe his least favorite meal on our first date that he'd turn out to be the person that would walk me down the aisle and hold my hand through fire and rain. "The man in my future" would find it in his heart to go beyond what he bargained for, put those wedding vows to the test, and empower others in doing so.

I believe in miracles for we have endured God's perfect storm. Prayer, the power of modern science, and Joe's easy willingness and deep desire to save his true love are why I am able to write this special letter.

When I first heard the good news that I was tumor free, I felt like I could fly. I am what the medical world calls "a miracle survivor," Dad.

I wouldn't have made it without you and Joe. You both have helped me understand how much I am loved. When you spoke from your heart and told me to believe in love and the power of a caring man, I did. I believed. You loved me unconditionally and then I found that same love from Joe. Because of you, because you were my dad, I knew what to look for.

I can still remember that morning I made my way into the kitchen after another sleepless night of questioning,

"Why me?" There you were, fully dressed as always, watching your favorite game shows on your Jazzer. You looked up and said, "MaryAnn, you look so beautiful today. No one would ever know you were sick." Later, when we were having dinner together, I tried to excuse myself from the table. That's when you said, "What's your hurry? Why don't you stay a little longer?" Then you smiled and added, "We never know how much time we have left."

Sometimes God makes His Presence known by giving us exactly what we need.

You died in your sleep that night.

My sadness of losing you was eased just a bit the next day when a knock on the front door surprised me with two beautiful birds of paradise that came with the note:

To my Daughter,
You were the gift of my life.

This reminded me that you were now in Paradise, with Dustin and Mom. And it reminded me to believe in miracles. How could I not? You just sent me flowers from Heaven for my birthday.

A small miracle took place as my oncologist reviewed the most recent MRI images of my brain and said that my tumor was gone.

As long as I keep looking, the miracles will keep coming. I know this, Dad, because of you.

ARTHUR "ARTIE" LARSEN
October 26, 1926 ~ January 25, 2014

⸻⸺ ৎ ⸺⸻

Every love story is beautiful but my parents' is my favorite. It all started back in 1947 at the opulent Prospect Hall on Prospect Avenue in Park Slope, Brooklyn. My mother, Theresa Powierski, was attending a dinner dance to welcome home her brothers and all servicemen in the Brooklyn area and celebrate the end of WWII. It was truly a magical night, a night to be remembered. It's the night my mother met my father, Arthur James Larsen.

Dad was seated across the ballroom with his buddies. As he lifted his cherried Manhattan to toast and thank God for sending him home safely, saying "Here's to you, Lord, and to life!" he was blindsided by my mother's presence. There was Theresa in a blue-jeweled gown with her  mother, Amelia Powierski, and her sisters. They were dining across the room. Call it what you like, destiny or God's mysterious plan, but as soon as he saw her he extended his toast, so to speak, and announced: "You see that girl over there? That's the girl I am going to marry!" Then he set down his Manhattan after taking one last sip for luck, walked over to my mother's table, and asked for her hand to dance. At that moment the bandleader and trumpeter started singing and playing, "There I've Said It Again." It was the first of many dances.

He eventually moved his beautiful bride to Prospect Street in Park Slope, Brooklyn. Dad said it was all one big coincidence that everything kept happening "on Prospect." I never believed him. To me, Dad was just that nostalgic.

I don't know if Dad believed in love at first sight before he met Mom, but he sure did after. I've always been a believer, or at least hopeful. My views on love mirror my feelings toward music. I didn't know I'd be lucky enough to experience both so fully. As a young woman, I'd always thought: *Gee, it'd be nice to find what my parents have.* But I had my voice. I knew how precious that was. How much luck is one girl allowed to experience?

So I focused on becoming the best I could be at singing. I found love later, by accident. Maybe I found it at the limo shop where I first met him. Maybe it was when he rejected my offer to go to the opera with me (when he was with his first wife). Or maybe it was when I cooked for him. Thank God the way to his heart wasn't through his stomach.

Luck hasn't follow me everywhere; that's an understatement. But Joe has.

I've always said I'm not a strong person. I'm just a jazz singer. We artists aren't generally motivated by money or power. But Joe keeps saying I'm tough because of everything I've gone through. After surviving the greatest loss a mother could ever face, and two brushes with death, I don't know if I'm tough, but I've come to embrace what it takes to make a change—if not all at once, then little by little. There's a lot of grace in the old saying, "One day at a time."

It remains to be a long road ahead, but I travel that path with purpose, a brave heart, and honesty, because that is the only way to transmit my true colors to the world. It's the only way for others to see what I have seen, and for them to believe in what I now believe in: The power of love.

But if it is true that I am tough, it's not because I've survived tragedies and am defying the odds, it's because of my own love story. It didn't happen "on Prospect," like Mom and Dad's, but that's the only difference.

A NOTE FROM JOE

Precision Medicine

I DON'T NECESSARILY BELIEVE THAT it's one specific thing that saved my wife's life by sending her into remission. But I do believe that this experience happened to us because it was supposed to. This was part of our life path together. I'm not just a numbers guy. I'm a big picture guy, too. I believe our journey was intended to be shared. I believe others can benefit from some of my investigative work and MaryAnn's strength and story of success.

THE DIPLOMAT HOTEL
HOLLYWOOD, FLORIDA
May 2015

If you or a loved one has been diagnosed with cancer, it's important to understand all the treatment options available. Personalized medicine, the medicine of the future, saved MaryAnn's life. It took a lot of research and reaching out to discover we had options outside traditional medicine. The word cancer can be so physically and emotionally debilitating that people jump into *this* or *that* out of fear— whether it be surgery, chemo, radiation, alternative medicine, anything. I'm not suggesting something like resecting part or all of a tumor surgically is the right or wrong decision; I'm merely stating that there may be numerous options available to you and doctors may not tell you about them out of either ignorance or malice. There's time to investigate. Don't panic. I know that's hard to do. We panicked, too. But then we took slow, deep breaths, and exhaled.

We went through the denial, the anger, the praying, and numerous stages of self-pity before accepting what was happening but we never accepted the doctor's prognosis. And neither should you, no matter how bleak it is.

MaryAnn and I also discovered how positive attitudes can change almost any outcome. Panic and rash decision-making were not our allies. Once the attitude is in check, you need to get down to the business of educating yourself. Google the diagnosis and change your eating habits, if need be, immediately. Avoid sugar and dairy (try almond milk instead). Eat lots of fruits and veggies instead. Bring your body's PH levels as close to neutral as possible. Cancers thrive in acidic environments, which are caused by diets heavy in sugar. Limit your alcohol intake, too—I restricted MaryAnn to one 5 oz. glass per day. It doesn't matter if it's red or white, though red is a little healthier for you. Sugar ferments away in most dry wines, not sweet wines. Make it a priority to research the best doctors and hospitals specializing in cancer research in places beyond your local area. Stay calm, keep the faith, and believe in the power of positive thinking. These are some of things that have worked for us.

Ask yourself: Is surgery necessary right now, or can a biopsy be performed to remove enough tissue to be genetically sequenced?

Go for three or four "second opinions" and search out the hospitals that not only specialize in that field but also have advanced precision medicine facilities to do genomic profiling of your tissue samples.

Most university hospitals or advanced research facilities have this available.

Sloan Kettering: www.mskcc.org

MD Anderson: www.mdanderson.org

Weill Cornell Medical: www.geneticmedicine.weill.cornell.edu

Massachusetts General: www.massgeneral.org/cancer

Duke: www.dukecancerinstitute.org

Mayo Clinic: www.mayoclinic.org

Dana-Faber/Brigham and Women's Cancer Center: www.brighamandwomens.org/bwhcancer/default.aspx

Seattle Cancer Care: www.seattlecca.org

Johns Hopkins: www.hopkinsmedicine.org

Many other health institutions across the country have these facilities.

If you happen to have surgery at an institution that does not have the facilities for genome sequencing, then have your doctor send your tissue samples to Foundation One (http://foundationone.com). Check with your insurance company first to see if you're covered. It's not as expensive as it was a few years ago, but coverage helps.

Be aware that the hospital is going to throw a sweet load of paperwork at you. When they do, look for the document asking you to donate your tissue to science. There should be three options in that document from which to choose. Make sure you select the option that research can use the results of their genetic testing, but that you will benefit from it, too.

I learned much from doing this research. I learned that many hospitals do not have the facilities to genetically sequence one's tumor, and some utilize the services provided by Foundation One. We were lucky that Sloan Kettering had the facilities. If you're not so lucky and your hospital doesn't, don't sweat it. Have your doctor send your tissue samples to Foundation One and have them do what they do best—genetically sequence it for the genetic mutations that could have caused your cancer to grow.

Once the molecular makeup of a tumor is broken down at the DNA level, oncologists are able to match the mutated growth with the relevant targeted therapeutic options. Treatment becomes specific to the patient's needs, not just generic cancer treatment.

Don't rely on doctors for all the answers. Become educated.

Once the mutation has been identified go to: https://clinicaltrials.gov and search to see if there is a clinical trial in your area.

Your doctors will probably have identified the available trials, but you never know. Some doctors/hospitals are reluctant to lose the money that comes with patients and may recommend staying on the typical cancer therapy regimens of surgery, radiation, and chemotherapy.

I can tell you right off the bat that if you live in a rural area, you probably won't find a clinical trial near you. Pharmaceutical companies need large participation in trials, meaning hospitals in more populated areas will get that business. At that point you're going to have to make a decision to pack up and hit the road. Most trials are pretty intense in the first few months, but after that you could get away with monthly visits.

The genomic profiling of your tissue may result in several mutations. MaryAnn had three, two of which were very common in GBMs. We decided to go with the mutation that was not common in GBMs. It was a blessing that there was a clinical trial at Memorial Sloan Kettering in NYC specifically for that third, less common mutation. She started in that trial two years ago, May 2014. Her prognosis was eighteen to twenty-four months in November of 2013, but through the grace of God, and the help of precision medicine initiatives, MaryAnn is now tumor free. For how long? I don't know. Doctors say cancers have an 80% chance of coming back.

Keep your faith, eat a healthy diet, keep a positive attitude, and exercise. By all means, exercise. MaryAnn's doing P90X now, and she loves it!

———— ∽ ————

What we traditionally refer to as "modern medicine" has been developed from the last fifty+ years of research, but it uses chemotherapies to treat cancers in a particular area of a body. Today's newest technology uses genomic profiling of the cancer cell—from one cancer patient's tissue across many known mutations—to fight the cancer with treatment options targeted to that mutation, not its place of origin.

Comprehensive genomic profiling cancer tests, such as the ones FoundationOne performs, provide the information your physician needs to help guide a tailored treatment approach using targeted therapies. You and your doctor can use the results from Foundation One to discuss possible treatment options, including FDA-approved targeted therapies, or novel targeted treatments under development in clinical trials.

Talk to your doctor about comprehensive genomic profiling and learn how you may benefit from a tailored treatment approach.

Massachusetts General Hospital (MGH) is also on the cutting edge of this science, as is Sloan Kettering. www.mskcc.org/cancer-care/risk-assessment-screening/hereditary-genetics/genetic-counseling

Harvard School of Medicine is associated with MGH.

www.massgeneral.org/pathology/research/resource-lab.aspx?id=74

The Bungalow Foundation (www.TheBungalow.Org) is a 501(c)(3) started by MaryAnn and myself.

The Bungalow Foundation is a Public Charity that funds bio-medical Precision Medicine Initiatives by way of grants to post-doctoral and clinical research fellows working with academic, medical, or research institutions. Our objective is to fund the research in an effort to expedite the discovery of a cure and develop treatments for different cancers by focusing on their genetic mutations—to treat the cancer based on its mutation rather than its location in the body. Basket Trials, as they are called, are trials that treat the cancer based on the cancer's mutation discovered through genomic sequencing. Go here for more information on Sloan Kettering's Basket Trials http://thebungalow.org/basket-trials.html

Immunotherapy is another component of Precision Medicine where a patient's own T-cells are engineered to target their cancer.

Through targeted identification of tumor biomarkers, genetic profiling and molecular characterization, vaccines, drug therapies, and other cutting-edge scientific discoveries may lead to new treatments and eventually a cure.

You can receive regular updates on the latest in cancer research and breakthroughs by subscribing to http://www.aacrjournals.org/ from the American Association for Cancer Research.

For additional information on personalized cancer treatment options, and our personal journey, check out the news sources below. MaryAnn's success story is working its way around the globe, creating awareness and offering hope.

Time Magazine, March 30, 2015 issue:

http://time.com/3750523/the-cancer-gap/

NPR "Living with Cancer" Series:

http://www.npr.org/sections/health-shots/2015/03/26/394327128/why-doctors-are-trying-a-skin-cancer-drug-to-treat-a-brain-tumor

NBC Nightly News with Lester Holt, August 20, 2015 News Segment on Treating Cancer:

http://www.nbcnews.com/health/cancer/new-kind-cancer-study-shows-tailored-treatment-saves-some-n412436

Here's a great video on Genetic sequencing and clinical trials:

https://www.mskcc.org/videos/role-genetics-clinical-trials

Music therapy is becoming increasingly more accepted in the treatment of cancer patients. Playing relaxing music for patients and engaging them in musical activities can assist in coping with fatigue, pain, and depression—common side effects of cancer treatment. In music notation, the coda symbol indicates a return to a specific place in the score. Often found at the end of a piece, the coda redirects the musician to play an additional passage of music, instead of ending the song. In this same way, music can help cancer patients navigate through their treatment—to return to a happy place in their mind, rather than think about the end of life.

THROUGH

Fire

AND Rain